P9-DGJ-341

Twayne's United States Authors Series

Sylvia E. Bowman, *Editor*

INDIANA UNIVERSITY

John Peale Bishop

JOHN PEALE BISHOP

By ROBERT L. WHITE

University of Kentucky

Twayne Publishers, Inc.   ::   New York

MANUFACTURED IN THE UNITED STATES OF AMERICA BY
UNITED PRINTING SERVICES, INC.
NEW HAVEN, CONNECTICUT

For
ALLEN TATE
who
first pointed out to me
the extent of Bishop's accomplishments

Preface

THE PLAN of this study of John Peale Bishop is simple. After a brief introductory chapter, there follows one which examines Bishop's critical essays—in order first of all to point up the intrinsic merit of his criticism, but also, and more importantly, to indicate the relevance of the criticism to an understanding of his poetry and fiction. Then follow chapters which treat in detail Bishop's published and unpublished fiction and poetry. The chapter dealing with the criticism is organized thematically, but chronology is the chief organizing principle of the fiction and poetry chapters. The third chapter, on Bishop's fiction, is almost twice the length of the criticism chapter; and the fourth, dealing with the poetry, is nearly three times as long as the second. The relative length of the chapters is an indication of my estimate of the importance of Bishop's criticism, fiction, and poetry.

In preparing this study, I have relied heavily on the John Peale Bishop papers on deposit in The John Foster Dulles Memorial Library at Princeton University; from them I have quoted frequently and at some length. I have also quoted extensively from Bishop's published works, more so than is common in literary studies of this sort. I have done so for three reasons: first, Bishop's works are all out of print and generally inaccessible; second, I have deemed it wise to support my generalizations and critical judgments by frequent reference to the texts under consideration; third, it is my belief that an author is always best represented by letting him have his own say—not even the most judicious paraphrase can convey the flavor and force of an author's original utterance.

NOTE: After initial footnote citations, I have located most subsequent references to Bishop's work parenthetically within the text, employing for this purpose the following set of abbreviations:

BP   Bishop Papers on deposit at Princeton
AD   *Act of Darkness*

CE   *The Collected Essays of John Peale Bishop*

CP   *The Collected Poems of John Peale Bishop*

MTG *Many Thousands Gone*

UG   *The Undertaker's Garland*

SR   "Some Unpublished Poems of John Peale Bishop,"
      The Sewanee Review (Autumn, 1963), 527-37.

ROBERT L. WHITE

University of Kentucky

Acknowledgments

For permission to quote from copyrighted works I am indebted to several publishing houses: to The Cambridge University Press for passages from Jessie Weston's *From Ritual to Romance;* to Doubleday & Company, Inc., for a passage from *South: Modern Southern Literature in its Cultural Setting,* edited by Louis D. Rubin and Robert D. Jacobs; to Farrar, Straus & Company, Inc., for a passage from Edmund Wilson's *The Shores of Light;* to Harcourt, Brace & World, Inc., for a passage from Horace Gregory and Marya Zaturenska's *A History of American Poetry;* to The Johns Hopkins University Press for a passage from *Southern Renascence,* edited by Louis D. Rubin and Robert D. Jacobs; to New Directions, Inc., for passages from *The Crack-Up,* edited by Edmund Wilson; and to The Oxford University Press for a passage from M. L. Rosenthal's *The Modern Poets.*

Lines quoted from "Cape Hatteras" are from *The Complete Poems of Hart Crane.* By permission of Liveright Publishers, N. Y. Copyright © R, 1961, by Liveright Publishing Corporation.

Quotations from the following works of John Peale Bishop are used by permission of Charles Scribner's Sons: *The Collected Essays of John Peale Bishop,* edited by Edmund Wilson (copyright 1948, Charles Scribner's Sons); *The Collected Poems of John Peale Bishop,* edited by Allen Tate (copyright 1948, Charles Scribner's Sons); *Many Thousands Gone* (copyright 1931, Charles Scribner's Sons; renewal copyright 1959, Margaret G. H. Bronson); *Act of Darkness* (copyright 1935, Charles Scribner's Sons).

"The Hours" (copyright 1941, *The New Republic*) is reprinted from *The Collected Poems of John Peale Bishop,* edited by Allen Tate, with the permission of Charles Scribner's Sons.

The personnel of the following libraries did much to assist me in my researches: The John Foster Dulles Memorial Library at Princeton University, The Lilly Memorial Library at Indiana University, The University of Minnesota Library, and The University of Kentucky Library. I am particularly thankful to Miss Sue Green and Mrs. Juanita Jackson of The University of Kentucky Library.

For grants to defray research expenses, I am grateful to the Kentucky Research Foundation.

My indebtedness to Mr. Allen Tate and Mr. Jonathan Peale Bishop is twofold. Mr. Tate has permitted me to quote from his correspondence with Bishop; in addition, he has encouraged me in this project and has provided me with much valuable information. Mr. Bishop has given me permission to quote from his father's correspondence and unpublished works; he also assisted me by commenting upon an early draft of my first chapter.

Two of my colleagues at the University of Kentucky took time out from their own endeavors and kindly gave portions of my manuscript a thorough reading. For their suggestions and strictures, I am most thankful to Frederic Thursz and Arthur K. Moore.

Finally, I wish to acknowledge the extent of my indebtedness to my wife. Not the least of her contributions was her careful shepherding of the several stages of the manuscript through the typewriter, but I am perhaps most beholden to her for her valiant efforts to keep my thinking and my style on an even keel. Sometimes we battled over an opinion or a choice of words, but Marilyn was always on my side.

Contents

Chronology

1892   John Peale Bishop born May 21 in Charles Town, West Virginia.

1906-   Attended Washington County High School in Hagers-
1910   town, Maryland.

1910-   Extended psychosomatic illness. Began writing poetry;
1913   had poem accepted by *Harper's Weekly* in 1912. At end of period, briefly attended Mercersburg Academy.

1913-   Attended Princeton University. Wrote for *The Nassau*
1917   *Literary Magazine* and was intimately associated with Edmund Wilson and with F. Scott Fitzgerald.

1917   First volume of verse, *Green Fruit,* published.

1917-   Commissioned in the United States Infantry; served over-
1919   seas with the 84th Division and with the post-war occupation forces.

1920-   Took an active part in the literary life of New York
1922   City. Served as contributing editor to *Vanity Fair.*

1922   *The Undertaker's Garland* (Edmund Wilson co-author) published. Married to Margaret Grosvenor Hutchins.

1922-   Departure for Europe and extensive travel on the
1924   Continent, particularly in France and Italy. Association with Ezra Pound, E. E. Cummings, and Archibald MacLeish.

1925-   Brief return to New York. Further contributions to
1926   *Vanity Fair* and employment with the New York office of Paramount Pictures. Hard at work on a never-to-be-published novel, *The Huntsmen Are Up In America.* Beginnings of his friendship with Allen Tate.

1926   Left the United States for a protracted sojourn abroad and took up residence in Orgèval, France.

1931   Won *Scribner's Magazine* short story prize for "Many Thousands Gone." Volume of short stories, *Many Thousands Gone,* published.

1933   *Now With His Love* (poetry) published. Final return to the United States.

1933- Lived for a short while in Connecticut, the home of his
1937   paternal ancestors; then in New Orleans. Began to contribute significant critical essays to the most important American literary journals.

1935   *Act of Darkness* (novel) and *Minute Particulars* (poetry) published.

1938   Moved into "Sea Change," a house built according to his specifications in South Chatham on Cape Cod.

1940   Served as chief poetry reviewer for *The Nation*.

1941   *Selected Poems* published.

1941- Served in New York City as publications director of The
1942   Office of the Coordinator of Inter-American Affairs.

1942   The anthology *American Harvest* (co-editor Allen Tate) published.

1943   Brief service, interrupted by illness, as Resident Fellow at the Library of Congress.

1944   April 4, died in Hyannis, Massachusetts.

1948   Posthumous publication of *The Collected Poems of John Peale Bishop* (edited by Allen Tate) and *The Collected Essays of John Peale Bishop* (edited by Edmund Wilson).

John Peale Bishop

CHAPTER 1

Introductory and Biographical

ABOUT TWO WEEKS before his death, John Peale Bishop dictated to his wife two four-line epitaphs. One of the quatrains was:

> Long did I live
> Consistent, lonely, proud.
> Not death, but fear of death,
> Restores us to the crowd.

The other was:

> Here far from the lovely land that bore me,
> By the cold sea I lie,
> Let none who have known love deplore me,
> The rest may pass me by.[1]

Taken together, the two epitaphs manage to convey something of the ambiguous, almost pathetic, quality of Bishop's life, and of the anomalous position to which his literary reputation has drifted during the generation that has passed since his death.

I *Lost Amid the Lost Generation*

In many respects, Bishop strikes one as a representative figure of the 1920's and 1930's. He published his first book of poems in 1917, his final volume of poetry in 1941. An expatriate who lived many years in Europe, he was also an editor of *Vanity Fair,* a poetry reviewer for *The Nation,* and a contributor of essays to the *Southern Review* and *Virginia Quarterly Review.*

He was intimately acquainted with such men as Hemingway, Pound, and Cummings and even closer to such friends as Edmund Wilson, F. Scott Fitzgerald, Archibald MacLeish, and

Allen Tate.[2] At the same time, however, Bishop was always more apart from, than a part of, the exciting climate of the 1920's and 1930's. While he had a rare gift for friendship, he struck many as aloof and distant, and he never fitted into any literary coterie or took part in any concerted movement. A Southerner sympathetic with the regionalist program of the Southern Agrarians, he never affiliated himself with their efforts to set up the antebellum South as a cultural and political ideal. As an expatriate, he was fully aware of the cultural ferment on the Continent but spent most of his time with his family in an old chateau in Orgèval, away from the hubbub of Paris and the Riviera.

In the 1930's, he refused to be drawn into any of the political alignments that swallowed up most American writers. When the *Partisan Review,* in the summer of 1939, staged one of the first of its many symposia, Bishop gave this answer when asked if he thought his writing revealed "any allegiance to any group, class, organization, region, religion or system of thought," or if he conceived it to be "mainly the expression of [himself] as an individual?"

> I have always believed that literature should oppose to any system, no matter how perfectly conceived, the "minute particulars of mankind." The mind craves nothing so much as a closed system, and the writer's mind is no exception; and yet he should, at whatever cost of violence, constantly set against any system, which at the moment is approved, the spontaneity and variety of life. In no other way can he bring his conscience to rest.
>
> All authentic writing comes from an individual; but a final judgment of it will depend, not on how much individuality it contains, but how much of common humanity.[3]

Because of Bishop's alienation from the cliques and causes that engaged his contemporaries, and because he devoted himself to the "spontaneity and variety of life" in a prideful but non-flamboyant manner, he remains a shadowy figure. He was never a spokesman and not ever a figure so idiosyncratic and spectacular that he could become a symbol. He was not a Hemingway or Fitzgerald or Tate; he was, however, a writer of genuine excellence. And, even after one takes into consideration his isolation and refusal to be part of a crowd, it is difficult to account for the lack of esteem with which he is now regarded.

Bishop, of course, has not been entirely forgotten. His critical essays on Fitzgerald, Wolfe, and Hemingway continue to provide insights for the student of American fiction. And Bishop has achieved a niche in literary history as a consequence of his Princeton friendship with Fitzgerald and because Bishop was the model for Tom D'Invilliers, the "awful highbrow" author of "passionate love-poems" in *This Side of Paradise*.⁴ When the two were at Princeton together, Fitzgerald was in the habit of jokingly referring to himself as Dr. Johnson and to Bishop as his Boswell. Ironically enough, Bishop's fate has been more and more to become Fitzgerald's Boswell—but a twentieth-century Boswell whose own accomplishments have gone unrecognized.

The bulk of his criticism seems nowadays to go unread, in spite of Edmund Wilson's hope that the essays as a group would make "an immeasurably stronger impression than—scattered, many of them, in periodicals of limited circulation—they ever did when he was alive" (*CE*, xi). Bishop's novel, *Act of Darkness*, and his shorter fiction have been almost completely overlooked. Most literary histories and critical discussions of American fiction ignore Bishop; if, as occasionally happens, his name does crop up in the index of a work, one generally finds, upon flipping the pages over, nothing but a string of titles and a muddled generalization.⁵

Allen Tate, when introducing a selection of Bishop's poetry to British readers in 1960, had this to say of Bishop's accomplishments and of his diminished reputation: "These books [the volumes of fiction and criticism] are the work of a mind of rare distinction. He was one of the best literary critics of the twenties and thirties. None of these books, as well as the poetry, is remembered by the American post-war generation."⁶

Mr. Tate possibly overstated his case, but not by very much. Bishop is frequently excluded from anthologies which give space to poets of much inferior stamp (for example, the most recent edition of Louis Untermeyer's *Modern American Poetry* omits Bishop while including the work of such third-rate poets as William Rose Benét and Lizette Reese). Bishop's name is as infrequently encountered in discussions of modern American poetry as it is found in histories and surveys of American fiction. For example, neither Louise Bogan in her *Achievement in American Poetry* nor Roy Harvey Pearce in his *The Continuity of American Poetry* mentions Bishop at all. And when a critic or literary historian does include Bishop in his discussion, he does so generally as an afterthought or in order to fit him into one of those lists of names by means of which the critic hopes to demonstrate his erudition and ability to generalize. For example, this is the solitary mention of Bishop in M. L. Rosenthal's *The Modern Poets: A Critical Introduction*: "And Jeffers, like Conrad Aiken, John Crowe Ransom, John Peale Bishop, and a host of writers all admirable in their several ways, has maintained a certain traditionalism in his art and thought—at a crucial cost, however."[7]

One would not wish to argue that Bishop's poetry has gone into total eclipse in America. His verse is included in several anthologies and textbooks of American literature, and a recent *Minnesota Review* essay on Bishop's work by Joseph Frank[8] may perhaps be viewed as a herald of renewed interest in Bishop's poetry. It should be pointed out, however, that Frank is an old admirer who published an equally valuable article on Bishop in 1947, and that only a single cursory article on Bishop's entire output and one explicatory note gave any attention to Bishop's poetry in the nine-year interval between the appearance of R. W. Stallman's essay on Bishop in the critical anthology, *Southern Renascence*,[9] and Frank's most recent article.

It is, of course, not impossible that Bishop's poetry deserves no more critical attention than it has received. It is even possible, as Horace Gregory and Marya Zaturenska ungraciously assert in their *A History of American Poetry*, that "no poet was ever more fortunate in his friends ... and their esteem for him often led to exaggerated claims for the talents he possessed."[10] It seems more likely—particularly in view of some of the other judgments to be found in the Gregory–Zaturenska book—that something other than friendship prompted Edmund Wilson's 1940 assertion: "The verse of John Peale Bishop is probably the *finest* poetic instrument that we have had in the United States since Pound and Eliot left. Trained in the great tradition of European poetry, his ear has a delicacy and precision which elsewhere have hardly survived.... He is perhaps the single American poet whose poetry is truly sensual."[11]

Bishop was, no doubt, a minor rather than a major poet; but he was, as Frank has argued, "that rare thing in American litera-ture, a true type of the second-order writer who, though incapable of supreme creative achievement, keeps alive a sense for the highest values." Frank then notes that it is "this type of writer whom the French delight to honor, recognizing their importance for the continuance of a vital cultural tradition."[12] Perhaps it is because America lacks any sense of "a vital cultural tradition," because Americans are constantly in the habit of forgetting their past and putting all their energies into the effort to remake their world with every new generation, that even Bishop's poetry is in danger of being passed over. For example, the recently issued (1961) critical anthology, *South: Modern Southern Literature in its Cultural Setting,* a re-vamping of *Southern Renascence,* once again includes individual essays on Robert Penn Warren, John Crowe Ransom, Allen Tate, and Donald Davidson; Bishop, however, along with Merrill Moore, has been dropped as a figure deemed worthy of separate treatment, and his name crops up only in an article attempting to define the peculiar nature of "Southern" poetry.

Perhaps even more indicative of the twilight that has settled over Bishop's poetry is the fact that Bishop is not once mentioned in R. K. Meiners' recent long explicatory article on Allen Tate's "Seasons of the Soul,"[13] a poem dedicated to Bishop's memory. One might think that any critic treating the poem extensively would consider the possibility that there might be allusions to or echoes from Bishop incorporated in the poem. Had Meiners been at all cognizant of Bishop's poetry, his reading of the "Autumn" section of Tate's poem would have been much less tentative; he would have recognized that this section echoes and parallels closely Bishop's "The Dream," which was published posthumously by Tate in the *Sewanee Review* in 1945.

Now, twenty years after his death, Bishop's self-proposed epitaphs seem dangerously close to proving themselves prophetically accurate. He has been too hastily restored to the crowd, and too many readers have passed him by. Perhaps those "who have known love" ought not to "deplore" him, but it is certainly not amiss to deplore the silence that has settled about him. And it seems not too extreme to suggest that readers who turn to him—to his criticism and fiction and, above all, his poetry—will obtain from him a heightened sensitivity to love, the major theme of his work, and to the powers and delicacies of art, that art by which he strove to redeem love from the inevitable ravages of time.

II *Sojourner from the South*

The circumstances of Bishop's birth and youth prefigured the divisiveness and separateness of his later years. He was born on May 21, 1892, in Charles Town, in the border state of West Virginia. On his mother's side, Bishop was descended from Scotsmen, Englishmen, and Germans who settled in Virginia in the seventeenth and eighteenth centuries. He was very proud of his Scotch ancestry; when he was a boy he went through old histories and painstakingly assembled a copybook volume which he titled *Colonel Cameron: His Ancestors and Descendants.* Bishop's father, however, was a New Englander whose family had emigrated to Charles Town from Connecticut soon after the Civil War. Bishop was always more or less instinctively a Southerner, but he was deeply attached to his father, who died when he was nine; Allen Tate remarks that in his later years Bishop experienced keenly the "deep conflict of loyalties felt by many people in the border South from 1865 to 1914" and that he "more and more took imaginatively the part of his father, of the outsider, of the déraciné" (CP, xii).

The Charles Town of Bishop's boyhood sank deeply into his memory, to be transformed years afterward into the "Mordington" of *Many Thousands Gone* and *Act of Darkness.* In many ways, Bishop's youth must have resembled that led by most young boys of the upper middle class in small towns of the turn-of-the-century South; but Bishop was precocious in his intellectual interests and at the same time set back in school by an extended illness that made him several years older than his classmates when he finally entered Princeton. When he was still a child, his father taught him to paint, and until he was seventeen he planned to be a painter. He was also very much interested in botany and ornithology; two of his adolescent heroes were the painter-naturalist-explorers Audubon and George Catlin.

Bishop attended day school in Hagerstown, Maryland, and later went to the Mercersburg Academy, just across the West Virginia border in Pennsylvania. It was while he was at Mercersburg that he became seriously interested in poetry; notebooks and copybooks among the Bishop papers at Princeton show that he had been writing poetry steadily since at least 1910. The notebooks of 1913 include more than twenty poems fairly copied out, along with a chart indicating how the poems which he had begun sending out to editors were faring. Most of them were promptly returned, but *Harper's Weekly* accepted one of his offerings, "To a Woodland Pool," and published the poem on September 28, 1912, a full year before Bishop went up to Princeton.

Almost immediately after his arrival at Princeton, Bishop began publishing poems in *The Nassau Literary Magazine*. As Dean Christian Gauss has remarked in corroboration of Fitzgerald's portrait of Bishop as Tom D'Invilliers, Bishop stood out among the many bright young men who attempted to found an oasis for poetry and literature on the Princeton campus: "John looked the poet that he was. There was an air of distinction about all that he did. He came to Princeton with a more carefully thought out and more accomplished mastery of the technique of English verse than any other undergraduate of that talented group. Even as a freshman John had a self possession and self mastery which gave him the poise and bearing of a young English lord."[14]

Bishop's early collegiate verse was highly imitative, modeled on Shelley and Swinburne and the poets of *The Yellow Book;* but his precociously metrical ear in a few years became attuned to the French and Italian poets he studied under Gauss's direction, and in 1917 he published a slim volume of verse under the ironically modest title, *Green Fruit.* By the June of Bishop's graduation from Princeton, the United States had entered World War I, and Bishop accepted a commission in the infantry. Wartime experience did not affect Bishop's work so decisively as it influenced Dos Passos and Hemingway, but Bishop's encounter with death was to make itself felt in the nihilism of *The Undertaker's Garland* (co-authored with Edmund Wilson) and in the urgency of the love poems he wrote in the 1920's.

Upon his return to America after the war, Bishop plunged into the literary life of New York. From 1920 to 1922, he was one of the editors of *Vanity Fair*, where he was in charge of the weekly book page, and to which he contributed reviews, poems, and humorous sketches. By now, he was reading Pound and Eliot and more of the later Yeats, and was fully aware of all the new currents in modern poetry. Edmund Wilson, who was also on the staff of *Vanity Fair*, reports that during this period Bishop worked with "perfectionist concentration on his poetry—

which he recited in the bathroom in the morning and to which he returned at night."[15] Bishop, along with Wilson, had been one of Edna Millay's suitors in 1920, but in 1922 he married Margaret Hutchins. After their marriage, the two left for an extended sojourn in Europe.

While in the army, Bishop had seen little of Europe, but now he and his wife traveled widely. They spent much of the time in Paris and in Sorrento, where Bishop worked hard at his poetry and in study of the Provençal poets. In 1924 the Bishops returned to America, but only for a short stay. He found employment in the New York office of Paramount Pictures and resumed his contributions to *Vanity Fair;* most of his energies, however, were expended on an abortive novel, *The Huntsmen Are Up In America,* a novel that Scribner's encouraged but eventually declined. Bishop finally abandoned the project after Fitzgerald wrote him a long, detailed criticism of the book in support of his opinion that "It has occasional spurts . . ., but it is terribly tepid."[16] The collapse of Bishop's hopes for the novel only aggravated the dissatisfaction he had felt with the United States upon his return to the New York of the middle 1920's. According to Edmund Wilson, Bishop gave the impression of having "found America intolerable. He had no gift for advancing himself; he did not much enjoy the excitement of the twenties. The whole environment seemed a great deal more alien to him than Italy and France had been" (*CE,* x).

When Bishop and his wife escaped to Europe for the second time, they took pains to insulate themselves from the hordes of Americans who were invading France in the closing years of the boom. They bought the Château de Tressancourt in Orgèval, reputed to have been one of Henry of Navarre's hunting lodges, and settled down to a life of leisured domesticity. During these years they continued to make excursions to various parts of Europe, but three sons were born during this period, and the visitors whom they entertained were few. Allen Tate, who did visit them frequently, is of the opinion that Bishop was not entirely benefited by his remoteness from centers of literary activity, "that he had not been happy in that charming isolation. More dependent upon a sympathetic literary society than most writers, he seemed in that period remote and without concentration, except at intervals when he produced, in a burst of energy, a group of poems or occasional story" (*CP,* xiv). Bishop's isolation, along with frequent bouts of ill health, undoubtedly drained much of his energies, but he did manage to publish two books during his second stay in France. Scribner's brought out his volume of short stories, *Many Thousands Gone*, in 1931, and *Now With His Love*, his first volume of verse since *Green Fruit*, appeared in 1933.

Bishop's increased productivity in the years just after he and his family returned to America in 1933 tends to support Tate's feeling that Bishop's particular sort of expatriation had not been good for him. In 1935 he completed and published *Act of Darkness*, a novel which owes a good deal to his memories of the Charles Town of his boyhood. The same year he published *Minute Particulars*, most of the poems of which seem directly inspired by his renewed acquaintance with America. By 1935, after living for a while in Connecticut and then for a year in New Orleans, the Bishops had moved into "Sea Change," at South Chatham on Cape Cod, the house in which he wrote his last and most moving poems.

The life which the Bishops led at "Sea Change" was as elegant as that which they had known in the Château de Tressancourt. Edmund Wilson has noted that the house, "a special creation of Bishop's old Princeton friend, the architect William Bowman, had something of that lofty splendor which John always managed to summon." When the Bishops had guests, they "ate on Dutch marquetry chairs at a long Louis Treize table in a high coral-pink room with Venetian cupboards in the corners and windows on three sides that opened on the white-wicketed lawn and gave a view of the pale blue water" (*CE*, xiii). In describing his interests and tastes for Millett's *Contemporary American Authors*, Bishop wrote: "As to my tastes, I like to eat and drink, and above all to talk; I am fond of looking at paintings, sculpture, architecture and formal gardens; in a very modest way, I paint and garden myself. In particular, I like the architecture of humanism and the music of the eighteenth century. I prefer the ballet—at its best—to the theatre. I no longer care very much for reading, except for information."[17]

During the first three or four years of his stay at "Sea Change," Bishop produced little poetry and nothing of fiction (the partly biographical *Act of Darkness* exhausted his fictional vein). Then, two widely separate events late in 1940 and early in 1941 occasioned a renewed burst of poetry. The death of Scott Fitzgerald in December, 1940, prompted the elegy, "The Hours," and indirectly led to the troubled and noble poems of the last years of his life. And his acceptance of an invitation to come to New York to serve as the Director of the Publications Program in the Office of the Coordinator of Inter-American Affairs brought him into direct contact with the literary and public worlds he had for such a long time shunned. During these years, which saw the publication of his *Selected Poems* in 1941, he studied Spanish and translated Spanish poetry; worked hard at setting up a proposed *Pan-American Review;* and with Allen Tate edited the anthology *An American Harvest.* Mr. Tate, who saw him constantly during these years, has testified that "He seemed in the year and a half he thus spent in New York to regain something of his old enthusiasm for literature" (*CP,* xv).

Bishop's health had long been poor, however, and he was forced to go back to Cape Cod in the middle of 1942. In 1943 he went to Washington to serve as an aide to Archibald MacLeish in the Library of Congress, but a heart attack forced him to leave after two weeks. Seriously ill from then until his death, he was bedridden most of the time, but his renewed enthusiasm for poetry remained high even as his life was ebbing away; as long as he was able, he continued to work on poems whose publication he would never witness. During the last months of his life, however, he could do little work. Toward the end, he was hardly ever conscious; he died in the Hyannis Hospital on April 4, 1944, just when the birds were once more beginning to dart across the waters of Cape Cod.

CHAPTER 2

Bishop's Criticism

JOHN PEALE BISHOP did not publish a great deal of criticism, and the essays which he did publish promote no systematically developed set of critical theories. Edmund Wilson's edition of Bishop's *Collected Essays* runs to more than five hundred pages, but Wilson included nearly a hundred pages of previously uncollected and unpublished fiction; brief reviews take up another hundred pages. Bishop's fully elaborated essays occupy only one half the volume, and there are not very many of them—all told, about twenty-five. As Wilson notes in his introduction to the essays, Bishop was never a polemicist and was never comfortable as a journalist. He produced several delightfully witty essays during his New York days with *Vanity Fair* and two or three very good travel pieces, but he never seriously engaged in the sort of literary journalism which attracted such writers as Wilson and Malcolm Cowley. Because he was not vitally concerned with formulating and advancing literary and social reforms, Bishop never went in for programmatic criticism such as that practiced by Eliot and Pound, and later by Tate and Ransom. His essays certainly reveal a critical intelligence, but it is not one set on propounding doctrines and is rarely given to exhortation.

Because of the relative slightness of Bishop's critical output and because of the occasional nature of many of his essays, it is difficult to find in his non-fictional prose any consistently elaborated set of critical principles or any dominant pattern of themes and interests. When the essays are looked at as a whole, the result is, as Wilson notes, "not a series of literary critiques—though there are some admirable studies of literary subjects—but a set of discourses on various aspects of civilization: literature, painting, moving pictures, architecture, manners, religion"

(*CE*, vii). As a critic, Bishop might be compared to Wallace Stevens or William Carlos Williams, two other poets who produced reviews and occasional essays; but it would be much easier to demonstrate the organic nuclei within the writings of Stevens and Williams than to locate the thematic centers of Bishop's criticism. One has the feeling that Bishop wrote most of his essays because he happened to be, at the moment of composition, deeply interested in the topic under consideration—even if that topic had been proposed to him. This is not to say that the essays are inconsistent or that Bishop's convictions about art and society fail to make themselves apparent in his criticism. The essays do reflect the man, and from them one can begin to formulate something of Bishop's critical viewpoints. What is more, since most of the essays and reviews were written after 1935, they reflect his mature opinions, judgments which he had arrived at after two decades of experience and reflection.

Bishop's essays, and many of his reviews, are highly readable and worthy of close attention for what they have to say about their individual subjects; I do not, however, intend to discuss them individually or to take them up in their entirety. For, while Bishop is an excellent essayist and an astute critic, in the long run he is more important as a poet and writer of fiction. I propose, therefore, to approach his essays as if they were a series of conversations closely relevant to his fiction and poetry and to discuss only that material which bears most directly upon his concerns as a creative artist. Three particular themes which engaged Bishop throughout his career are to be considered: social and historical views, especially his criticism of modern industrial society and his uneasy attitude toward the South; his views of human nature and his speculations about religion and mythology; and his ideas about the nature and function of art.

I *The Traditions of Force and Form*

Like most of his fellow artists during the 1920's and 1930's, Bishop was unhappy with and critical of American culture. He objected to the callous brutality and ugly disorder of modern capitalism and industrialism. He was depressed by the hysterical repressiveness of American morality and upset by the dull mediocrity of American intelligence. Bishop, however, took little part in the various efforts launched by his contemporaries to reform American manners and to shape the American future. He contented himself with pointing out some of the historical factors behind the American cultural sickness and with drawing his compatriots' attention to the outlines of previous cultures in which he found much to praise and much to emulate. The whole of Bishop's work reveals him to have been an admirer of several cultures unlike that of America—of the ancient Mediterranean world of the Greeks, of Renaissance Italy, of the world of eighteenth-century Europe, of modern France—but in his essays he particularly alludes to France and the civilization of the eighteenth century as it took form on both sides of the Atlantic, particularly in the American South.

In 1941, while contributing to a symposium on "The American Culture," Bishop gave voice to his hopeful conviction that "the future of the arts is in America." He felt that the arts had an immediate future only in America because it was only here that intelligence could "pursue its inquiries without hindrance from the State and publish its discoveries unmolested by authority" (*CE*, 169). He was also heartened by the arrival in America of refugee artists and thinkers from Europe—heartened not so much by his awareness of the riches they might bring with them as by his sense that the emigrés might be able to give direction to the judgments Americans would be called upon to make if they assumed cultural leadership. For Bishop felt that Americans stood in danger of turning too inwardly upon their own shallow past and of insisting wrongly that American art should follow the narrow path of "folk art." Bishop distrusted the American habit of making popular taste the touchstone of esthetic criteria and he did not wish to see America turn away from Europe as it had done in the nineteenth century:

> For to tell the truth, folk art is all very well in its way, but its way is limited. And Americans have only exceeded those limits in the arts when, not ignoring Europe, they have come to a proper understanding of their relation to Europe. In the eighteenth century that relation was intuitively grasped and consciously understood, not only by those who gave form to our state, but by those who produced our only formal architecture. They were separated from Europe in space, but continuous with Europe in time. They were contributors to the one civilization they knew; it was not conceivable that they could belong to any other. (*CE*, 170-71)

In the nineteenth century, Bishop felt, America had been tragically cut off from Europe. Bishop was convinced that the history of the twentieth century was chaos, but he also believed that American artists had benefited from the erosion of American isolationism in the twentieth century and that his generation's renewed awareness of Europe and of the traditions of European art had been of immeasurable value. Bishop believed that in the 1920's the centers of civilization, those centers where, "in each art, the tradition can best be acquired and with it an intenser consciousness of one's own time" (*CE*, 172), had been in Europe and that the prime capital of civilization had been Paris.

By 1941, however, Paris had fallen; and Bishop sensed that "The actual center of Western culture is no longer in Europe. It is here. That, I believe, admits little question. The question is, can we provide that conscious center which the culture demands?" (*CE*, 172). Bishop only tentatively sets forth some guidelines for answering the question he has raised. He insists that "we must find a way to reconcile our own past with the vast past of Western civilization" and that "We must be Americans; but as artists we must remember that, before America was, we were men" (*CE*, 174). He does, however, lovingly celebrate the French civilization so recently overrun by German panzer divisions.

In Bishop's analysis, France had succeeded so well in its task as "arbiter of the arts and of all the attributes of civilization" partly because it had so nicely mediated between the North and South of Europe; France had to "admit the claims of two rival conceptions or civilizations and continuously to mediate between them. It was owing to her own fine and luminous genius . . . that she was able to consider both, to control both, to bring both into a single and harmonious whole." Bishop thought that French culture was exciting because the "human experience from which it is derived is exceeding rich and varied"; he also thought that French art was distinct from that of all other countries because of the French "passion for form. In France, the artist was allowed the utmost possible freedom in the choice of his material; he was praised in the end in proportion to his ability to unite force and form" (*CE*, 173-74).

For Bishop, as Joseph Frank pointed out some fifteen years ago, this need to reconcile the antagonism between "force and form" was "the key problem of modern culture."[1] In Bishop's view, France had effected a marriage between "force and form" by recognizing the insistent needs of the present while continuing to value the legacy of a traditional past—a past which in turn was forceful and alive:

> Nowhere was one more conscious of living in the present than in France, and yet there the present was continuously enriched by the past, and not the past of France only, but by a classical past which the French contrived to reconcile with their own. For, in insisting upon a logical structure, upon balance and grace, the French never forgot that these qualities, which we associate with classical art, actually are those of a living body at its perfection, the body which we derive from a remoter past than that of Greece. (*CE*, 174)

Bishop looked back with respect to the eighteenth century because the world of Jefferson and Voltaire provided him with images of societies where the instinctual life and tradition went hand in hand. Bishop was not a wholehearted admirer of the age of the Enlightenment, which he deemed to have erred in over-emphasizing the powers of rationalism; he knew that the eighteenth century had its ugly as well as its charming aspects. But he firmly believed that after the eighteenth-century social and cultural disintegration had set in: "The eighteenth century had hideousness and drabness to show no less than the nineteenth... But the age which Hogarth sets before us in such unenviable brutality had not lost the power to make beautiful things, and not only had their beauty a social use, but more than a little of their significance depended upon an assertion of a social order." Bishop knew that there had been social injustices in the eighteenth century, but he also insisted: "In a society where every man knows his place, he may have much injustice and discomfort to put up with, he may know all sorts of hungers and privations; he will still know the ground sound beneath his feet. Distress he may know, but not disintegration. His soul still has its mask of union on." (*CE*, 115).

Because Bishop was such an admirer of the civilization of the eighteenth century, he often praised the remnants of that culture in the American South. Bishop was well aware of the specific limitations of the Southern tradition—but he was attracted to his Southern ancestors because "theirs was a civilization of manners." He felt that only such a civilization could impose that sense of discipline and respect for form he deemed so necessary for human life. He respected his ancestors because the "sense of the earth was strong in them, so that they could not cultivate many illusions as to the ultimate improvement of mankind. But in the meantime, their manners gave them assurance and . . . they preserved integrity" (*CE*, 11). Bishop knew that there were skeletons in his grandfather's closet, but he continued to assert that, even after "we have heard the full scandal of statistics relating to grandfather, we still know, not only that he was alive, but that he had arrived at a manner of living somewhat more amiable than any other that has ever been known on this continent" (*CE*, 3).

Bishop granted that life in the Old South had been crude and provincial, and that after the eighteenth century its intellectual life became moribund; but he held that in the South there was more than the mere outline of a civilization: "For the South, whatever may be said, had at least passed those two tests which the French have devised for a civilization and to which they admit only themselves and the Chinese. It had devised a code of etiquette and created a native cookery" (*CE*, 4). Bishop believed that the Old South had "developed the virtues of an agrarian civilization," but he did not—as did most of the Southern writers who aligned themselves under the Agrarian banner in the late 1920's—insist overmuch on the possibility that moral and social virtue were intimately connected with agriculture. Instead, he called for "a symmetry between agriculture and industry" (*CE*, 12). For Bishop, the social order of the South depended not so much upon its agrarian foundation as upon the fact that its agrarian culture enabled the institution of the family, with its loyalties and means of conveying tradition and inculcating discipline, to prosper.[2]

As a man of the twentieth century and as a writer deeply concerned with the South, Bishop had to contend with what he termed "the myth of the Old South." Bishop knew that the mythic haze which so many Southerners had thrown over their past had falsified and distorted the actual conditions of Southern life and society; he was also quite cognizant of the fact that the very ancestors he so much respected had been sometimes prone to self-deception and romantic affectations. Bishop, however, did not high-handedly reject the Old South and the myth which had gathered about it. Instead, he grappled with that myth and found it was not altogether false. In a passage which describes the efforts of his generation of Southern writers to deal with their homeland, he neatly sets forth what he himself had concluded:

> And when they began to work among the mythical remnants of the Old South and got down to fact, what they discovered was a society which, though it constantly entertained romance, was severely classical. What they found was a social order which, though colored by the presence of African slaves, was very close to European society in the eighteenth century. It was not English, it was not French; it was, in fact, like nothing but itself. It had few cities. But as in provincial France before 1789, as in countrified England before the industrial revolution, society was still based on the family. Its structure was regulated by custom, as, though affected by climate, its speech and manners were maintained by tradition. (*CE*, 126)

Bishop decided that Southern writers were fortunate in having grown up with the myth of the South, for by means of it they "discovered a past which they could by no means altogether praise, but which was not without its power for truth." The ambiguous nature of this myth constituted no problem, for Southern writers "could oppose to it the 'minute particulars of mankind.'" The myth of the South could be used, "not merely in contrast to the present—both as that present belongs to the South and to other parts of the country—but in criticism of it. The Old South was a possible, a proved, form of life." Looking at the example of Faulkner, in 1939, long before his fellow Southerner had achieved critical acclaim, Bishop suggested that it was "because he is aware of what a Sartoris once stood for that Mr. Faulkner can recount to such bitter effect the conduct without honor and without shame of a Snopes. . . . It is this knowledge, won out of a myth, that gives Faulkner's words weight" (*CE*, 127).

Perhaps because of his own absorption in the Southern myth, Bishop tended to argue that no other region of the United States possessed a sense of tradition and identity with previous ages. He never, to be sure, suggested that New England and the Middle Atlantic colonies had not participated in the transatlantic culture of the eighteenth century. In one of the essays unpublished during his lifetime, he contrasts nineteenth-century

Newport with the old merchant community of the colonial period and turns back "in admiration to the shipowners" who had been superseded by the society dowagers: "They trafficked in human flesh, but at least they grew up. And they created on these rocky ridges a certain civilization, brief but native and something of a sport, like the fern-leaf beech, which grows nowhere but here" (*CE*, 426). But even as he commended the shipowners, Bishop suggested that Newport had more in common with Charleston than it did with the rest of New England: "Newport is in Rhode Island and hence in New England. But it long ago turned its back on both and looked south" (*CE*, 419). It pleased Bishop to think that Newport was not really a part of New England; for he had concluded that Puritanism, or what his friend Allen Tate called "the New England idea,"[3] along with America's ever-repeated frontier experience, were responsible for the decline of tradition in the United States.

According to Bishop, "New England is more than a section of the country; it is a peculiar spiritual climate" (*CE*, 298). Bishop agreed with Tate that the intense spirituality of Puritanism, as seen in the seventeenth-century divines and in such atavistic Puritans as Jonathan Edwards and Emily Dickinson, "had an immense, incalculable value for literature: it dramatized the human soul"; but he found even the earliest Puritans objectionable because they "set out to destroy tradition." Bishop held that the founders of the Massachusetts Bay Colony had given their descendants a "cast of mind" that was to determine the course of American history. In place of the "old dependence upon the arbitrarians of God," however, the men who succeeded the first Puritans began "to devise a doctrine which was later to be called self-reliance. It was they who have determined America, and they were, no less than their uncompromising fathers before them, enemies of custom" (*CE*, 6).

In spite of their antipathy to tradition, the Puritans and their offspring had, willy-nilly, continued to participate in Western civilization as long as they remained in the tightly knit communities along the Atlantic seaboard. But Bishop felt that the accelerated movement of Americans westward after the Revolution enabled them to realize, at bitter cost, their desires to throw off the bonds of custom and tradition: "The Atlantic did not cut America off from Europe; only the Alleghanies did" (*CE*, 426). Unlike most American writers, Bishop found little to praise in the American frontier experience and was highly suspicious of what Henry Nash Smith has termed the American "myth of the garden."[4]

Bishop found fault with the American pioneer because he felt that in the American West "the New England idea" had gone sterile and sour. Several times in his essays, Bishop repeated his belief that the American had reverted to savagery when he ventured beyond the protecting ranges of the Appalachians, but perhaps his most eloquent prose pronouncement on the pioneer is to be found in his address on the future of "The Arts in America":

> It was not the Atlantic that separated Americans from the European tradition, but the woods of the Old West. Even so, they came to the edge of the woods, aware of all the centuries they brought with them. It was only after the pioneer had gone a long time in that green twilight, where a man could march all day and never see the sun, that he left behind him, not merely the little settlements, in the clearings; he left behind him his age. In contact with the savage, he became the contemporary of the Choctaw and the Cherokee. (*CE, 171*)

In a critical essay dealing with Vardis Fisher's early novels about Idaho, Bishop remarks that "Americans have preferred to take a romantic view of the pioneer.... They have concentrated on the advance and not until lately minded its ruthlessness" (*CE, 59*). In Bishop's view, the frontier movement had led not only to savagery but also to a loss of intelligence and a desiccation of the human spirit. In Bishop's version of the frontier movement (the historical accuracy of Bishop's account is irrelevant; Bishop's historical views are of primary importance for what they tell us about Bishop—not about the West), New Englanders had been in the vanguard of the settlement of the Middle West. The pioneer sons of the Puritans had carried with them "a spiritual culture, and the Middle West had no other." Consequently, for the Bishop who believed that a vital culture had to reconcile both the demands of the spirit and those of the body, the Middle West became a "soulless region" (*CE, 298*).

In his most famous essay, "The Missing All," Bishop most completely examines the effects of the degradation of the New England idea in the Middle West. Bishop argued that Puritanism "had never provided the new country with a particularly satisfactory morality." Along the seaboard, however, where "it was counter-balanced by other forces, inherited decencies, values transmitted and transmuted," there had for a short while been a genuine culture, "rather cold, but flowering nevertheless in a lovely and inclement air." Once the frontier had crossed the mountains, however, the New England idea "began to go bad. It needed the strictness of the village, it demanded the sense of the community. Else it was disembodied." When the pioneer entered the green of the forest, "something of his intellectual toughness was shed." When he emerged upon the prairies, he was toughened and hardened and still had with him the Puritan distrust of nature, but it was now unrelated to his experience: "That hatred of death which is behind the Puritan hatred of life was still with him, but through varying vicissitudes was lost. The meaning of Puritanism is a contempt for mortality; in the Midwest it was forgotten." Bishop felt that as long ago as Mark Twain Midwesterners had come to the conclusion that the New England morality was inadequate, but he found it unfortunate that Twain, as well as the two Midwesterners he discusses at length in "The Missing All," Fitzgerald and Hemingway, could turn to no other morality than that "which had been shaped for him, as for all Americans, in Concord and by Walden Pond. The Midwesterner was self-reliant, he had a profound trust in the natural goodness, the sanctity almost, of unrestricted man" (*CE*, 70-71).

Bishop had little trust in unbridled self-reliance and the natural goodness of unrestricted man. For him, a civilization had to offer its citizens, particularly its young citizens, guidance in the form of "customs, courteous manners and inherited wisdom. While there is always much that a young man must, of necessity, face in complete nakedness without so much as a tatter from the past, it is not a very profitable way to go through life. It means an emotional impoverishment." Most Americans, Bishop felt, led such impoverished lives—led them because of the influence of the New England idea and the frontier experience: "It is because we are continually beginning the world again, every ten or fifteen years, that we wear that desperate look of youth. Ours is a mechanic's conviction that history is all bunk." It was because he felt that the South had not denied history that he could look back through the haze of the past and find, in the myth of the South, a society worthy of his praise. Remembering his own disillusionment in World War I, he envied what he regarded as the dedication to tradition that characterized the soldiers of the Confederacy: "They, at all events, had a tradition, which they carried with them and found as useful as a body-servant.... Their attitude toward life was alike, and when they faced death it was in the same way. This makes for integrity, as it certainly also makes for a sounder emotional life" (*CE*, 4-5).

II   *The True Religion of Mankind*

Bishop's views of human nature and human conduct might, at first glance, seem more than a bit inconsistent. Although he was hostile to Puritanism, and even though he was, as his friends have testified, a strongly sensual man with a "touch of eighteenth-century coarseness,"[5] he was not a libertine or a romantic egoist. He was hardly a Christian, but his essay on *Finnegans Wake* reveals him as a man who was convinced of the truth of the Christian account of the Fall. He had no convictions of the innate goodness of man, but he believed that man could realize himself only through expression of his native impulses. Bishop believed that man is simply an animal, and that the bases of human life are sensual and instinctual; for Bishop, however, it is paradoxically the transformations of man's animal nature that set him apart from other animals.

In the draft sheets of an essay which he never completed, Bishop underlines and praises the animal in man by asserting: "It is not by geometry, nor even more complicated mathematical systems, non-sensuous and wholly abstract, that we are set apart from other mammalians. It is precisely in those qualities which he shares with the animals that man has been most anxious to assert his humanity." Speaking metaphorically, Bishop observes that, since his expulsion from paradise, man has sought "every means to distinguish himself from the animals—thought, geometry, philosophy, science, religion." At the same time, however, man has strived with as much vigor to demonstrate that "he differs most from the animals in all that he shares with them. Hence he invents love. He becomes a cook." For Bishop, "the amorist on his bed, the gastronomist at the table, both are assertions of human dignity" (*BP*).

While Bishop was convinced that man was essentially animal, he also insisted that man was unique: an animal capable of giving shape and order to his life, one capable of intelligent self-consciousness and one gifted with the opportunity to realize his sensuous experiences through the forms of art. Bishop would have man praise the arts because "they show us that ours is a sensuous world which no animal shares" (BP). He felt that "we must live from the instincts, for the mind unsupported not only cannot tell us how to behave, it cannot give us any very satisfactory reasons for living at all"; but he also believed that "the instincts demand a discipline. Else they are distrusted" (CE, 9-10).

Bishop had no desire to revert to "the paradise of leopards and elephants" which man had known before he achieved self-consciousness, but he nevertheless held that "the whole history of civilized man is nothing else but a continuous magnification of the animal called man" (BP). Because of his conviction that the impulses of civilization had their springs in man's animal nature and because he felt that the arts and traditional disciplines had as their function the "magnification" of man's animality, he was at odds with the New Humanist position of Irving Babbitt and Paul Elmer More. To Bishop, the New Humanism was a stunted offspring of Puritanism: "in part a counsel of exhaustion and in part a pathetic nostalgia for the small-town morality of an older America, dominated by the thin spire of the white meeting house." Bishop argued that Babbitt had misrepresented the counsel of "Aristotle and others of that violent race, who never, in their clear-sightedness, supposed . . . that a mild happiness was the end of life. What we ask is not repression of passion, but a discipline that will in controlling it also conserve it" (CE, 10-11).

In the uncompleted essay from which I have quoted above, Bishop develops his argument with Babbitt at greater length. He is most unhappy with Babbitt's notion of decorum as central to morality. He prizes decorum as much as Babbitt does, but for Bishop it is not to be arrived at by a timid and prudent morality: "Decorum is that state toward which all passionate action and only passionate actors move. It is life brought to formal beauty; underneath the most savage passions may, nay must surge."

Bishop agrees that man, in order to prove himself man and not merely animal, needs to shape and control his life, but he insists that "the control which leads to decorum is like that of the poet, not that of a Coolidge. And moreover it is always passion in control that produces both form in living and form in art." For Bishop, passion was all-important—particularly sexual passion. He also felt that man could affirm his unique dignity only by admitting to, and attempting to give form to, his sexuality. He abhorred the sexual prudence he discerned in the preachments of the New Humanists and he concludes his rebuke of Babbitt by calling attention to the metaphoric dimensions of human love:

> Consider for one moment the art of love, which is the type of all the arts, and consists in the completest stimulation of desire consistent with a control which falls just short of complete. There must be passion, else there can be no love, there must be heat and violence; but there must also be mastery up to that point where in poetry the lines begin to write themselves, and all is under the control not of the poet, but of the words, as sound and sense, which he has already written. That is to say, in living as well as in any of the arts, there is a place for excess, a moment when prudence must be surrendered, and nothing is held back. Only so can the most completely satisfying results be achieved. (*BP*)

It was undoubtedly because of his deep-rooted conviction of man's basic animality, coupled with his refusal to accept the explicit doctrines of Christianity, that Bishop turned to a sympathetic exploration of the implications of mythology. In 1935, Allen Tate argued that Bishop's attempt to utilize the Christian myth in some of his recent poems had not been totally successful, that it was a strained effort "to replace our secular philosophy, in which he does not believe, with a vision of the divine, in which he does not believe either."[6] After the publication of his friend's essay, Bishop sent to Tate several closely typed pages of "Notes on the Note." After admitting that he could not believe literally in the Christian myth, he observed: "The divine toward which I struggle, obscurely and haltingly, is the divine that is manifest in Mozart as clearly as in Jesus." The divinity which Bishop perceived and groped for could make itself manifest only in "human experience, the man temporarily made god, that is, relieved from the limitations of time and space." Bishop admitted that Tate had all but convinced him that he would be better off if he dropped the Christian myth, but then added ruefully: "The trouble is, the myth is so much a part of our experience; it is very hard to get rid of, even when no longer believed in" (*BP*).

Fortunately for his later poetry, Bishop did not accede to the advice which he presumed Tate to have given him. He did not abandon the Christian myth, but continued to employ it in conjunction with other mythologies out of man's past—and in much the same way that he was able to employ the cultural myth of the Old South, and for much the same reasons: because of his conviction that a writer, by means of myth and mythologies, could come into contact "with the common mind and make its resources of feeling and sentiment, its depths of desire, his own" (*CE*, 125). Bishop turned to mythology for two other, but still related, reasons. Like Yeats and Eliot, he believed that mythology could supply the artist with the symbolic representations which he felt were a permanent necessity of poetry; furthermore, he believed that ultimately there was more than a germ of truth in the great mythologies.

Rejecting both the formalities of modern religion and the pretensions of modern science, Bishop came to the conclusion that only art could adequately describe man's relations to the universe in which he found himself. Bishop admitted that relations between the earth and the sun could be presented mathematically, but he vehemently avowed that "no mathematician in the world can find an appropriate symbol for my relation to the sun, or the earth even for that matter" (*BP*). Bishop thought that mythology could provide the symbols to express such human relations and he felt that the mythology of the past, if its implicit truths were grasped, could be meaningful to modern man. In an unfinished essay on the artist as mythmaker, he observes that "Christianity in its great period had wisely avoided being explicit except on one subject and that, its cosmogony, which it had derived, I believe, from secular sources, was to prove its vulnerable point. The rest is myth, ceremony and symbol. But if these could be interpreted, or rather be translated into terms accessible to our needs, then it might be that they will speak to us" (*BP*).

Bishop attempts, or rather lays the groundwork for, just such a translation in his most important non-literary essay, "*The Golden Bough*," published in 1936, long before the current awakening of interest in "myth and ritual." Bishop opens his essay by noting that *The Golden Bough* is a not too covert attack on the assumptions and presumptions of Christianity—that Frazer's tracing of the lineage of the rites of Nemi is designed to bring out the correspondences between Christianity and paganism and thus to demonstrate that the former is not at all the unique and other-worldly religion its devotees have assumed it to be. Bishop argues, though, that Frazer has not so much undermined Christianity as he has "revealed what one may in all simplicity call the true religion of mankind" and that it is possible for men of the twentieth century to feel that Christianity, as a result of Frazer's prodigious researches, "has gained as much as it has lost." Christianity could now be seen as a religion "extending its existence into the dark backward and abysm of time," thereby gaining "not only the respectability of age, but another authenticity. . . . It is shown as a heritage, not from Judea and Greece only, but from the earth." Christ could now be seen as a god akin to other gods, but Bishop concludes that "He is not less divine because of the company of Adonis, Osiris and Thammuz. His divinity is to be found in precisely those attributes which he shares with these and other older incarnate gods" (*CE*, 27-28).

When Bishop, aided by Frazer's anthropological compendium, looked at the long history of Christianity, it was borne in upon him that "its central mystery is the Mass" and that the Mass, when closely analyzed, "turns out to be a symbolic presentation of the eternal relation of man to a living and sustaining earth" (*CE*, 28). For Bishop, this celebration of life and man's dependence upon the earth, as symbolized in the mystery of the Eucharistic Mass, was the great glory of the medieval Church. He was repulsed, however, by what he took to be an opposing tendency within Christianity: the asceticism which he took to be more an expression of despair and affliction than the "acceptance of death as fulfillment which comes to strong men when life is at the full" (*CE*, 29). Bishop's late poetry makes it quite clear that he would have no part of the ascetic impulse within Christianity, but he is as much a celebrant of the life-giving and life-redeeming features of Christianity as is Henry Adams: "The fearful gaze of the gaunt statues at Chartres becomes the radiant look of the smiling angels at Rheims. And that change is accomplished with the recovery of the active will and the beginnings of a more stable society. From then on, and until the springtide is past, the Mother of God lifts for adoration the body of a child, reborn as god; laments over the body of the god, dying as man" (*CE*, 30).

While Bishop could reconcile himself to much in Catholicism, he could admire very little he discerned in its rebellious offshoot, Protestantism. Writing in the 1930's, Bishop observed that the generation of the 1920's had been looking for a "new consciousness"—for, in effect, a "religious consciousness, if religion may be understood to be a lively and communicable sense of the powers superior to man which control the course of nature and of human life." For Bishop, a denial of the existence of such powers was unthinkable; what was unfortunate, to Bishop's mind, was the fact that only a "scientific account of them as natural forces" was available to his generation and that the scientific accounts were hardly satisfactory. Bishop, who was of the opinion that "America was a creation of the Protestant mind," also looked upon modern science as the handmaiden of a specifically Protestant mentality. He admitted that Protestants in the seventeenth and eighteenth centuries had been moved by religious considerations, but he found it pathetic that the Protestant churches had rejected the central ritual of the Mass— "the essential mystery of Christianity"—and had thereby deprived "Christ of His powers as a God" (*CE*, 31).

Bishop acknowledged that science had enabled man "to project a superior order upon the heavens," but it was his conviction that science was not able to relate man to the "ampler heavens" which its superior instruments had mapped out (*CE*, 33). Science had projected a dream of progress, but Bishop felt the dream had gone awry: "the applications and derivations of scientific thought . . . have brought into our lives an unparalleled disorder" (*CE*, 34). To the proposition that what is needed to cure the world's disorder is more science, Bishop brought a profound scepticism. Science was not an adequate replacement for a living mythology for two reasons: first, "order in a living society cannot conceivably be of the mechanic kind"; second, he deemed unsatisfactory the scientific concept of time—because it derived "from the contemplation and measurement of space" and therefore was not one "by which men and women, subject to decay, can live." Looking at the promises and failures of science, Bishop could hazard an estimate of "why myths have suddenly become so important to us. It is because through them we see mankind in time" (*CE*, 35).

Assessing the course of Western history, Bishop observed: "It was the triumph of the European mind, in its youth and spring-time of thought, that it was able to adapt the Christian myth to its needs and, extending the human drama to include, not merely lives, but conceivable centuries, to endow it with shape and meaning." He could agree that the next tide-swell in the history of Western man, the scientific and Protestant revolt that had gathered its forces after the Renaissance, had imparted an im-measurable impetus to the human spirit and had "resulted in an unprecedented conquest of space." But he was also convinced that "that movement has now spent itself. It lies gasping with its own success, like Alexander when he had trampled Europe, Asia, and Africa."

Bishop had no proposals for a religion to replace the outworn pretensions of modern man, and he seems not to have enter-tained any hopes for a return to primitive mysteries (he could only scoff at the metaphysical pretensions of Marxism and he would probably have hooted at Joseph Campbell's suggestion that science itself may provide the materials for a new my-thology[7]). But he did remind his fellow men that religion "may attain an even nobler form than any Frazer has set down. . . . There is the religion of Saint Augustine and Dante, in which the gods are no longer propitiated save by conformity to their will." It saddened Bishop to realize that an age conditioned by scientific determinism could no longer fully comprehend Augustine's testament of acceptance; Bishop insisted, though, that "even in a deterministic age, we are plagued by the necessity of conform-ing to our destiny, and the problem remains of according desires with fate" (*CE*, 35-36).

III *The Discipline of the Artist*

While Bishop could sympathize with, and find much to celebrate in, the mythological aspects of Christianity, he sus-pected that a devout commitment to Christian belief handicapped poets, particularly modern ones. In 1940, when reviewing the work of the young Catholic poet, Raymond Larsson, he remarked: "It is really very hard for a poet to be a Christian. For though we think of so many of the great poets as having been religious, the realms of poetry and religion are not the same. The essential relation to Christianity is that of man to eternity, while in poetry

the relation that must always appear is that of man to time."
Bishop believed that the poet could not always easily accept "the
moral values which the Church, seeing beyond time, places on
human conduct. Poetry does not see beyond tomorrow and
tomorrow" (*CE*, 322).

It is true that Bishop did not envision a wholesale return to
mythological religion and that he did not propose any replacement for outmoded religious beliefs, but he did prize art as a
human activity which could enforce and uphold values similar
to those which mythology and religion had once made central
to human life. It would not be accurate to say that Bishop proposed to set up art as a substitute for religion (he believed art
and mythology to have come into being together at the dawn of
man's conscious history), but he did think that art could be
meaningful in the modern world in a way that formal religion
could not be—and it would be accurate to suggest that, for
Bishop himself, art had become the single human activity to
which he could entrust his faith and hope. In his uncompleted
essay on the artist as mythmaker, after speaking of the accomplishments of such men as Yeats, Joyce, and Lawrence, he observes: "They were artists. But art is the only means left us to
describe the relation between man and the outer world. Mr. Eliot
has quarreled with putting art in the place of religion; but art is
the only means left us to present the complete man in relation
to all that is not man" (*BP*).

Earthly time was important to Bishop, as we have seen, because of his conviction that man was essentially animal, and
consequently mortal. Near the end of his active life, while
appearing on the New York City radio program, "Out of the
Ivory Tower," he summed up his beliefs about man's nature and
the function of art when he remarked: "The very essence of
being a *man* is to own a poignant and inescapable conviction of
being a creature of time. And the essential task of *poetry* is to
display man in relation to time."[8] In the radio interview, Bishop
was restating a theme to which he had turned repeatedly in his
critical essays. In "The Discipline of Poetry," he points out that
all the various arts strive "to present the conflict of man with
time. This is as true for those arts, like architecture, which we
ordinarily call spatial, as it is for those arts which, like music, are
strictly temporal. And the famous release which the arts afford
is essentially a release from time." Bishop observes that the arts

of the Orient apparently provide such a release by transporting the beholder or listener into a mystical state in which "there is no longer an awareness of time and its duration"; in Western art, however, the artist effects the release from time "by an assertion of control." Bishop knows full well that man cannot really control time; it is his argument, though, that what man can control, "if he is an artist, is the consciousness of it" (*CE*, 104). In another essay, "Poetry and Painting," he puts forth a similar proposition: "The exhilaration and the calm which is produced by art is due to the sense it gives of release from the conditions of living, not by its denying those concepts without which life is to us inconceivable, but by controlling them. Only through the means of art can the conviction be created that man controls time and space. It is in the means of art, then, that we must look for its end" (*CE*, 180).

Bishop's concern for the "means of art" is evident in practically all of his criticism and essays on the various arts, and this concern makes his criticism pungent and his own approach to art radically different from mere formalism or elegant estheticism. His concern for the techniques of art amounts to a stern morality. He sees the poet as a man who must control the sense of time by the only means at his disposal, the sounds of words: "it is upon their sensuous disposition that he must depend to convey a sense of duration." The painter, restricted to spatial effects, must depend solely upon the application of paint to canvas if he wishes to create an "illusion of enduring space" (*CE*, 176). The minds of the artists may engender "conceptions of time and space" at variance with the technical means at their disposal; but Bishop, who took as a sign of cultural disorder the conscious efforts of artists of the twentieth century to confuse and merge the arts (even though at times he himself was one of those artists), felt that the essential nature of his art confines the poet to "the conventions of time," just as the art of the painter "holds him to a conventional space. The mind is free; but it is the mind of a condemned man" (*CE*, 183).

Because of his conviction that the artist was a man condemned to labor within the bonds of his craft, Bishop could state: "In criticism of the arts, the technical approach is often the most profitable. It would seem that in this, as in other serious inquiries, the proper question is *How?*" He admitted that such an approach might overlook "the very secret and essence of the art," and that it was an unpopular approach. As an artist himself, however, he found not at all scandalous or inane Renoir's observation about Velázquez' "The Maids of Honor": "All painting is in the pink ribbon on the dress of the Infanta" (*CE*, 14). In the long run, if not in the end, it was the mastery of craft which Bishop most admired in the work of his fellow artists. In his essay on Hemingway, after remarking that Hemingway's "vision of life is one of perpetual annihilation," one where "Eternity . . . is in love with the garbage of time," Bishop concludes with words of genuine homage, not altogether inapplicable to Bishop himself:

> What is there left? Of all man's activities, the work of art lasts longest. And in this morality there is little to be discerned beyond the discipline of the craft. This is what the French call the sense of the *métier*. . . . In *The Undefeated* [sic], the old bullfighter, corrupt though he is with age, makes a good and courageous end, and yet it is not so much courage that carries him as a proud professional skill. It is this discipline, which Flaubert acquired from the traditions of his people and which Pound transmitted to the young Hemingway, that now, as he approaches forty, alone sustains him. He has mastered his *métier* as has no American among his contemporaries. That is his pride and his distinction. (*CE*, 45-46)

Bishop's absorption with the problems of the artist as craftsman was a natural consequence of his larger concern with the over-all problem of form in art. For Bishop, artistic "form" was the order which the artist imposed upon the disorder he found in nature and in human history—the means whereby the artist was able to structure the forces to which he was necessarily enthralled. In discussing the historic significance of Paolo Uccello's great painting, "The Rout of San Romano," he observes that the murderous maneuvers of the combatants have been brought under the total control of the painter. In the actual battle, the gestures of the soldiers were necessarily "violent," but in the painting "the impression they convey is one of absolute calm. Man has been added to nature. The order of art has been imposed on human disorder" (*CE*, 177). Elsewhere, while somewhat uncomfortably introducing a group of surrealistic "chain-poems," he remarks that the unconscious, when it makes its way nakedly into poetry, is not necessarily very interesting: "What is interesting in a work of art is to have what it offers to the conscious mind brought completely under control and made subject at once to a sensuous discipline and a moral order" (*CE*, 304).

For Bishop, both the *content of form* and the *form of content* are essentials of a great work of art. That is to say, even though Bishop might insist that "It is in the means of art ... that we must look for its end," he was not sympathetic with the tendency in modern art to make artistic means ends in themselves. He felt that the efforts of the French symbolists to write "pure poetry" had been a pursuit which led away from poetry because it led away from human experience: "It led at last into a region as remote as it was deserted, for it lay beyond the confines of human experience. The air there was very pure indeed, but it could not be breathed" (*CE*, 98-99). In like fashion, he felt that the revolutionary program of modern abstract painting had been necessary to clear the ground of nineteenth-century sentimentality, but he deemed pure abstractionism in painting incomplete and unsatisfactory. Bishop argued that there was "an art beyond the art of such painters as Matisse," even though he could honor Matisse as an artist "who introduces an order into what is most disorderly about us, our sensuous life, and who therefore deserves all our moral admiration." The other rank of artists, where Bishop put Picasso, is made up of "those who, for lack of another word, must be called poets. These enable us to contemplate the spectacle of human destiny with passion and with calm. We see, and are moved, it may be profoundly moved; but we are serene" (*CE*, 200).

In spite of his distrust of pure abstractionism, Bishop did not think that mere potency of content could guarantee integrity to a work of art; the content itself had to possess a center and a valid structure. Bishop cites both Thomas Wolfe and Hart Crane as examples of artists who lacked this sense of form. Of Crane in general, he remarks that "all his astonishing felicity with words cannot hide his failure in content. A poet's best phrases are almost always spontaneous, but spontaneity will never account for a poem" (*CE*, 304). Of Crane and Wolfe together, he observes: "Both had what we must call genius; both conceived that genius had been given them that they might celebrate ... the greatness of their country. But Wolfe no more than Crane was able to give any other coherence to his work than that which comes from the personal quality of his writing."

Following Allen Tate's speculations as to the factors involved in the failure of *The Bridge*, Bishop hazards the guess that both Wolfe and Crane were handicapped by their failure to find, or create, a myth adequate enough to infuse their work with meaning: "There is no idea which would serve as discipline to the event." Unable to avail himself of the fruitful resources of myth, Wolfe was thrown back on his personal sense of experience and was unable to escape from the immediacy of the moment. In Bishop's opinion, Wolfe possessed intelligence but, because of the circumstances of his career, would not trust to his intelligence. Consequently, he was not able to endow his fiction with the form that is meaning. Writing in 1939, Bishop concluded that *Of Time and the River* reveals Wolfe to have been a man of indubitable talent, but that the faults of the novel are "fundamental" and not due "merely to an excess of fecundity." The fundamental fault, in Bishop's opinion, is an absence of form—not merely in the novel, but in Wolfe's thinking about the materials of his fiction: "He did not find for that novel, nor do I believe he could ever have found, a structure of form which would have been capable to giving shape and meaning to his emotional experience" (*CE*, 131-33).

In addition to his stress upon form as the meaningful center of a work of art, Bishop gave much attention to its complementary aspect: the actual structure of the perceived elements of the art work. The two aspects are intimately related, but Bishop was wary of notions of creativity which suggest that form may spring automatically from the inner content of the work of art: "Form does not grow out of the material, though a given material may immediately suggest an appropriate form" (*CE*, 376). That Bishop would have liked to entertain such notions of organic form may be inferred from some of his private comments on Tate's "A Note on John Peale Bishop," in which his friend had remarked that the modern poet "struggling to get hold of some kind of meaning, blunders into the *impasse* of form."[9] Bishop says: "The sense of plastic form, the obsession of unity (which Mozart had), has that not disappeared from everything? Our structures are intellectual and deliberately imposed." Bishop feels that an instructive parallel may be drawn from a comparison of modern engineering and earlier architecture: "Architecture also depended on exact knowledge and on *numbers,* as does engineering. But after knowledge there was growth and finally flowering. The engineer puts forth no buds" (*BP*).

Bishop confessed that what he should like to find was "a form which would impose itself," but he also admitted: "I have never found it. I doubt if the age has" (*BP*). In spite of his desire for such an imposed form, he would not go along with thinkers such as Emerson who believed that enthusiasm alone could guarantee a satisfactory resolution of the problem of form. Just as he insisted that passion under control, or just on the verge of control, was necessary in the art of love, so he insisted that careful craftsmanship was necessary in shaping and ordering the completed work of art. In one of his aphorisms, he calls attention to Apollo's "bisexual countenance" and goes on to observe that this bisexuality has particular meaning for the poet: "The vigor and daring of the poet should be employed at the moment of conception. The elaboration should be carried out with delicacy. The male should engender, the female complete, the poem" (*CE*, 373).

And in his essay on Wolfe, after insisting that "the meaning of a novel should be in its structure" (*CE*, 131), he then makes his most careful statement about the duties of the artist as craftsman and about the relationship between inner meaning and external structure of the work of art: "The intellectual labor of the artist is properly confined to the perception of relations. The conscience of the craftsman must see that these relations are so presented that, in spite of all complications, they are ultimately clear. It is one of the conditions of art that they cannot be abstractly stated, but must be presented to the senses" (*CE*, 134).

Bishop's concern for form and his insistence upon the sensuous nature of art make themselves felt most strongly in his comments upon the techniques of verse. Given Bishop's passion for form, there was for him no such thing as free verse. He felt that a poem by its very nature made use of—worked against the resistance of—the limits of form: "The one freedom which is allowed the poet is the possibility of expanding or contracting these limits." If the poet abolishes the notion of such limits, he loses "not only the chief advantage his craft allows him, but his fecundity. In art, as in love, nothing is more sterile than limitless desire" (*CE*, 104). Bishop believed that "The purpose of the poet, as of the race, is to assure a progress in time. What we call the living quality of a work of art is precisely this: that it

endures, continually changing, without ceasing to be itself"
(*CE*, 20).

In order for a work of art to achieve such life it had to achieve
form, and after long thought Bishop felt it was possible to formulate two tentative "laws" about the nature of poetry that
would distinguish its particular formal structure: "*Poetry is such
an arrangement of words that their real qualities take precedence
over their arbitrary ones. Poetry is such an arrangement of statements that their arbitrary pauses take precedence over the real
ones*" (*CE*, 17).

The first law deals with the tension between the signific and
the connotative elements of language. Bishop could not look with
complete favor upon the efforts of the surrealists to write poetry
from the depths of their unconscious, for he felt that the surrealists had lessened their power "in surrendering the intellectual
potency of the word." Bishop could, however, sympathize with
their "protest against those who would rather not remember that
words are combinations of sounds as well as means of conveying
ideas" (*CE*, 304). When he speaks of the "arbitrary" qualities
of a word, Bishop refers to the meanings and etymologies "which
will be found assigned to it in the dictionary." By "real" qualities,
he means those which are "perceptible to the senses, with all that
implies of accent, quantity, consonantal and vowel conjunction."
To these physical qualities of the word, the poet must add "all
the sensuous and emotional associations which the word may
carry for him. . . . They distinguish his style from that of another
poet and upon their richness and intimacy much of his merit will
ultimately depend" (*CE*, 17).

For Bishop, poetry was meaningful. Its meaning, though, was
not that of prose, and neither were its means. In order to achieve
its ends, it needed to make full use of the symbolic and sensuous
resources of language. As one of Bishop's aphorisms puts it, "The
poet does not explain. He illuminates" (*CE*, 369).

Bishop's second "law" for poetry is a bit more complicated.
Believing as he did that the essential problem facing the artist
was the control of time, he felt that the poet needed to introduce
into his work a temporal measure, and that "the means which the
poet uses to that end is verse" (*CE*, 104). Bishop thinks that in
all good poetry there are two patterns at play. One pattern is
that dictated by the syntactical structure of the poet's statements;
the pauses dictated by the syntax of the poem are the poem's

"real" pauses. The "arbitrary" pauses are those which the poet, employing his sense of form, superimposes upon the poem's basic syntax. Bishop notes that these arbitrary pauses "may or may not coincide with those pauses which the sense of his statements would dictate; but at all events they take precedence over them" (*CE*, 365).

Bishop was not greatly impressed by the efforts of modern poets to write poems based solely upon syntactic structure. Of Amy Lowell's poems, "written as she said in cadence, which means simply that she allowed phrases of her sense to determine the phrasing of her sound," he remarked: "the gratification is small; now that the charm of their irregularity is gone, her compositions have only a slight interest and that not inconsistent with prose" (*CE*, 18). Bishop argues that the good poet "is attracted to verse because of the resistance it offers him" (*CE*, 102). By accepting the resistance of "verse" (a term which Bishop uses to designate the arbitrary pauses of the poem), the poet is able to give fullness and actuality to his statements.

The pauses which the poet introduces into his text "bring to the passage of poetic time a seeming necessity. They give it an objective reality, in which we can, as long as we are willing to accept the convention, believe." Bishop holds that only "a rhythm marked by recurrent accents or their equivalent can give us this immediate perception of time." Although he felt the need for meter or its equivalent in poetry to insure poetic movement, he did not think that movement could be "simply measured and made to pause at predetermined and completely arbitrary intervals."

In good poetry, he felt, there was always a struggle between the statement and the verse, "a contest between the rhythm and the meter, and upon that complication a good deal of the quality of the poem depends" (*CE*, 104-5). If the poet avails himself of all the resources of poetic language to resolve that struggle, he is sometimes able to substitute "another time for that in which we live and are destroyed." Bishop's praise of Verlaine's "Clair de Lune" indicates full well his respect for such an achievement: "He has created another time, and one not measured by the calendar. It is in this sense, possibly in this sense alone, that the poem can be called a creation. To achieve it has required the full resources of an art" (*CE*, 20).

Bishop's critical comments on art and poetry are, I think, even more fruitful than his speculations on history and religion. It should be pointed out, however, that all of his critical thought was consistent: all of it was concerned with the problem of "continuity in the midst of change" (*CE*, 105). It should also be remarked that Bishop was not so much motivated by a desire to formulate critical schemes as he was driven to grapple with the underground forces of human life and human art. In his notebooks he confesses that more than once he had tried to shut himself "within a system" so that he might "preach at [his] ease." He could never rest within such a system, however: "always something spontaneous and unexpected, out of the fullness and universality of life, arose to give the lie to my knowledge.... I could change or extend my criterion as much as I wanted, always it was too slow to catch up with the infinite variety of man."

If Bishop had any basic theory about the imperatives of human conduct, it was that man had to avail himself of the legacy of the past and that the artist could not afford to cut himself off from the hard-won traditions of form and craftsmanship. Bishop's involvement with the past, however, was not a retreat from the present; he knew well that "the effort to conceive the present as a continuous past will add to, not decrease, the burden." Bishop thought that the prime task facing modern men and modern artists was "to restore memory—if necessary, since only here and there does it persist in the Western world, to re-create it." Anthropology and archeology could assist in such a task, but Bishop felt that it was essentially "a labor of the imagination." He respected scholarship and theory-makers, but he was primarily an artist—one with a proper awe for the sensuous and passionate in man. It was his devout belief that "only those whose life overflows... can hope to make the dead live again" (*CE*, 377-79).

CHAPTER *3*

Bishop's Fiction

AMONG the "Aphorisms and Notes" which Edmund Wilson included in his edition of Bishop's essays are several staccato comments on "Why the novel is what it is": "A *middle-class art form*. Appears first with rising middle class. In England first. Aristocratic forms of writing: romance and poetry. Being middle-class, it is concerned with things" (*CE*, 384). Bishop had great respect for the novel as an art form, and a high regard for the accomplishments of such prose masters as Flaubert, James, and Hemingway; but perhaps it would not be amiss to suggest that both the slightness of his fictional output and the flaws of his fiction arise from the fact that he could not always manage to control and integrate his aristocratic tendencies toward romance and poetry.

For the most part, Bishop's fiction is starkly naturalistic, but he was not always at ease in this mode. He was never altogether happy with the novelist's concern with things as things, and the temptations of romance were so strong that he was frequently in danger of being lured into the land of Cockaigne. Except in one instance, he was unable to fuse the naturalistic and romantic modes. Furthermore, Bishop could not consistently provide his fiction with an artistically satisfying form, that form which he felt the novel genetically lacked because of its middle-class origins. Immediately after the publication of *Many Thousands Gone* (1931), Allen Tate wrote Bishop a congratulatory letter which also squarely pointed out the handicaps his friend had to overcome when he turned from poetry to fiction: "You have a *feeling for rhythm by phrases*, but not sentences, and your whole interest is *emotion not action;* and your interest in the emotion is its immediately perceived value, not for the sake of a dramatic situation but *morally.*"[1]

After the limitations and defects of Bishop's fiction have been noted, however, one should remark that his weaknesses are most evident in his earlier fiction and in his unpublished novel. For the most part, Bishop's published fiction exhibits both versatility and skill. *Act of Darkness* (1935) suffers from a lack of form, but its sensuous and sensitive language is hardly ever vitiated by an out-of-control poeticism. And *Many Thousands Gone*, even if its stories tend toward the static, is a remarkably integrated and successful volume.

I *Uncollected and Unpublished Fiction*

Although Bishop's most significant fiction is to be found in *Many Thousands Gone* and in *Act of Darkness*, several other stories deserve more than a passing glance. And the unpublished novel (one chapter of which Wilson printed in the *Collected Essays*) contains such brilliance and casts such light on some of Bishop's other fiction and poetry that it would be inadvisable to dismiss it as a totally wasted effort.

Two stories which Bishop published early in the 1920's nicely point up his contradictory impulses toward romance and realism. The realistic "Resurrection" was one of Bishop's contributions to *The Undertaker's Garland;* the romance "Porphirio; The Delicate Prince" was published in *Playboy* in 1923. "Resurrection," the concluding story in *The Undertaker's Garland,* is quite different in spirit from his verse contributions to the volume. As Joseph Frank has remarked, it is "uncluttered by the pseudo-macabre bric-à-brac marring his other efforts,"[2] free from the poses and affectations of his too consciously iconoclastic and too imitatively decadent verses. It is a simple story, almost slight, which graphically reports the reactions of a young lieutenant, in charge of a prisoner-of-war compound after the war, to the disinterment of an American soldier hastily buried during the battles for the Argonne. The officer, in order to demonstrate his toughness to the brutalized men under his command and to reassure himself of his grit, watches the corpse being dragged from the clayey soil—and grows sick and faint at what he sees. Bishop's description of the removal of the body is brutally matter-of-fact:

> Archer saw first a knitted sweater, still intact but soppy from the putrefaction beneath it. A clayey brown rag was over the face. The taut wire pulled again, sharply; something broke near the throat and a greenish blue substance, like a fowl's ordure, crumbled and fell over the sweater.... The cadaver began to

lift itself from the grave. The jointless head fell back, thickening the greenish ooze on the neck; the uneven arms spread out with each jerk of the wire, hunching their slimy sleeves. In the space where the thighs divide a glinting puddle of muck had seeped through the breeches cloth. The legs trailed woodenly.[3]

The insistent fact of the continuing death of the soldier's body—the "new life" which it has acquired "in its very putrefaction"—is, of course, in ironic contrast to the title of the story. The body, however, is not merely a sign of mortality; the rotting corpse and the sultry, scarred landscape which encloses it become for Archer symbols of "all the rotting desolation which filled the world" (*UG*, 184-85). When he thinks of the delegates to the peace conference at Versailles, of the "fashionable people" thronging the streets of Paris, and of the Y.M.C.A. "holding boxing bouts at the Palais de Glace, to provide the American soldiers on leave with wholesome and moral amusement," he perceives that they all represent "a desolation no less complete than the abrupt height of Montfaucon, and the hillside under it pitted with open graves, empty now as tombs of the resurrection" (188-89).

There is social and political and religious desolation in Paris, but Archer goes on to realize, after his nausea has passed, that Paris is also a city of life: in Paris "whatever was left of life ran at the full." His intimate glimpse of death is followed by a healing vision of Paris in the spring: "The sunlight came to the streets strained through a green net of leaves, and the night would be filled with lights and amorous voices.... Nothing was left but the fine vigour of his body, still young, and beginning to stir with heat from the liquor he had drunk." Against the fact of death, the story asserts the fact of life, of youth and sensuous existence. At the end of the story, Archer leaves the tent to which he has sickly fled: "And straightening his body he felt the sun warm on his face and hands, and the light of May burnished his uncovered hair" (189-90). Archer's emergence from the tent is the genuine "resurrection" of the story—a resurrection achieved only after recognition and admission of death.

"Porphirio," very unlike "Resurrection," is an account of the betrothal negotiations and marriage rites of a young Roman prince who discovers, to his bitter anguish, that there is truth in what one of his aged counsellors has to say about "Love"—that

"In action, it is brutal, soporific, sudorific, rapid and mephitic; sometimes in the young it is also strongly carminative" (*CE*, 472). As a youth, Porphirio had never laughed, being unable to comprehend the lusty pleasure with which his father and his father's courtiers responded to the antics and grotesqueries of freaks and clowns; but laughter finally breaks from him on his wedding night. A lone guard, passing beneath the bridal chamber, is mystified to hear "from the Prince, leaning on the night, long and long, bitter passionless laughter" (478).

Whatever may have been Bishop's intentions, the laughter which closes the story is weakly hollow—for two reasons: first, since Bishop fails to follow the prince and his bride into the nuptial chamber, the laughter is merely proclaimed, not concretely accounted for; second, and more important, the prince's laughter is all but swallowed up by the sensuous details of the palace and of the wedding ceremonies. It is quite obvious that Bishop in this instance is not so much interested in plot and character as he is in the story's opportunities for lush description, the quality of which may be seen in this passage detailing the ritual robing of the prince on his wedding day:

> The Prince remained a long time in his bath, which was filled not with water but with a distillation of wood-violets especially diluted by the Court Perfumer. Emerging at last like a dawdling wind from a garden, he was rubbed dry on a towel offered for the occasion by the Guild of Wool Merchants; and his toenails were pared with a knife presented by the Lord Mayor of Toledo. . . . The Prince was trembling when he put on his white leather pumps (with low silver heels) and the hat of crushed violet (starting into an ostrich feather), and violently trembling when at last he drew on his mantle, which enclosed him like a silver sheath. (476)

The sensuousness of the prose, as well as several details of the story, is highly reminiscent of Fitzgerald's fantasy, "The Diamond as Big as the Ritz"; but Bishop's story differs radically from Fitzgerald's in that his sensuosity is merely narcissistic. The lush prose and lavish descriptions are not the main thing in "The Diamond as Big as the Ritz"; by means of its fantasy the story makes an incisive comment on American character and society, if not on human nature in general. In Bishop's case, the mannered prose and the exotic descriptions serve no other end than self-display: "Porphirio" is hollow because it is all erudite glitter and not much substance.

Bishop wrote several stories dealing with Americans abroad but published only one, "The Fireplace," in *Story* in 1933. "The Fireplace," a slight effort, is a deftly handled and warmhearted tribute to the sometimes exasperating graces of that French civilization which Bishop so much admired. Nothing much happens in the story. An American couple moves into a Paris apartment, agreeing to retain a cook who is highly spoken of by their landlord. Georgette provides them with excellent meals, but refuses to be budged from what she thinks is the proper hour for meals. Her employers try to suggest an earlier breakfast, but "Georgette was not to be moved. As a cook she provided perfection, but she was to be persuaded neither to hurry nor economy. She knew how things should be done."[4] The Americans wonder if she is ever flurried or flustered until one morning she rouses them from bed with shouts that the fireplace is on fire. She rushes off for firemen, who finally arrive and eventually put out the fire, but only after they have ogled the American woman in her negligée and after their chief has written down on report forms complete biographical data on the two Americans. The firemen finally leave, roguishly saluting the wife on their way out; and the cook announces breakfast, at the exact time she always serves it, even though she apologizes for being unable to serve it at the usual spot before the fireplace. Once again, the Americans have been beaten; and the French passion for exactness and order is triumphant.

Civilized graciousness is totally absent from "A Man Who Thought," published in 1935 in the first number of *The Southern Review*. This story, which resembles nothing else Bishop ever wrote, is a tavern monologue by a New York shopkeeper who, finding himself consumed by hatred for his wife, plans to kill her by shoving her beneath a subway train. He lacks the nerve to carry out his plan; but, when the wife afterward dies in a traffic accident, the shopkeeper is guiltily troubled by feelings of inadequacy which come from his awareness of his own moral cowardice. In its command of vernacular idiom and in its portrayal of the muddled mentality of the lower-middle-class narrator, "A Man Who Thought" could well brook comparison with some of the stories of Ring Lardner and Nelson Algren. The most impressive feature of the story, however, is its nightmare vision of New York—a city of dead souls lost in anomie and imprisoned in their own corruption. The narrator and his wife had lived near the old Third Avenue "el" and the shop-keeper tells of his midnight disgust when the trains thundered by: "And when the trains came along past the window people would be sitting in the cars, being drawn along I don't know where. But they were awful in that light, their skins white and dead. And I thought they are just sitting there with their eyes open, being drawn along, growing nails and hair, not doing anything else but what corpses do in the ground."[5] The appropriateness of *The Southern Review* as a showcase for Bishop's story is readily apparent; "A Man Who Thought" is a not too subtle attack on urbanization and the machine-centered culture of the North. The New York of the story is overwhelming in its bigness and mechanical might, but it fails to provide its citizens with any purpose or to make their lives meaningful. The city is merely a monstrous embodiment of "force" and its inhabitants are as surely steeped in putrefaction as the corpse of "Resurrection."

Death, either physical or symbolic, is a central theme of most of Bishop's fiction. His third, and best, uncollected story of the 1930's, "Toadstools are Poison," published in the *North American Review* in 1932, deals with the confusions a very young child experiences when his Negro nurse takes him to witness the public hanging of a Negro who has poisoned his wife. The child has overheard the kitchen conversations of the servants, and he believes that the "Pleas Scott" who is to be hung is the same "Scott" who is a yard servant down the street. When the boy and the nurse, hurrying home after the hanging, meet the yard man the child is frightened and dumfounded.

The two most impressive features of the story are the successful manipulation of the difficult point of view and the portrayal of the Negroes' reactions to the murder and the hanging. In its command of point of view, "Toadstools are Poison" is fully as successful as Faulkner's "That Evening Sun," which was printed in *These Thirteen* in 1931 and which may have influenced Bishop. In both stories, the angle of vision is that of a child, but many years have lapsed between the events of the story and the telling of it. Such a strategy enables Faulkner and Bishop to utilize vocabulary and syntax beyond the reach of a child, while at the same time permitting them to employ vocabulary and syntax suggestive of a child's way of seeing and thinking.

The advantage gained by such a technique is offset by the artistic need to remain true to the point of view. In "That Evening Sun," the Quentin of memory is nine years old, but Bishop chooses what is perhaps an even more difficult point of view, that of a three-year-old. He carries off the trick very well, however, and the resulting prose is at the same time poetic and precise. Here, for example, is a paragraph describing the Negro whom the boy thinks is going to be hanged:

> He was a little nigger and very old. His clothes were old. His black felt hat had no brim and he pulled it on the back of his head; two holes were cut in the crown. His hair was grey, and he wore on his chin a little beard like a goat's, but crinkled, for after all he was black. He was shrivelled and black and dried up like those bunches of grapes that stayed on the vines after the leaves were fallen or brown. One eye had been bored by a cow's horn and was blue and blind. The other bulged and could see, the ball bloodshot and strained. (CE, 492)

Although Faulkner may have influenced the narrative technique of "Toadstools are Poison," it would be ridiculous to suppose that he is similarly responsible for Bishop's insight into Negro psychology. Bishop's portrayal of Negro life must be a consequence of his understanding of the Negroes he had known so intimately during his boyhood in Charles Town. In "Toadstools are Poison," the Negroes are not just characters with peculiar habits, dress, and speech (though Bishop manages very well to convey the flavor of Negro speech); he is able to reveal them as human beings who become intensely aware of life at the moment when death confronts them so terribly and so closely. The child-narrator of the story is not aware of what is going on about him, but his account of his nurse and her lover at the crisis of the hanging clearly reveals their essential humanity: "I wanted to see and turned my head to Ellie. She was smiling like something hurt her and looking straight ahead. John Harris was behind her. His face was very black, and there was sweat on his cheeks. He held her, his arms coming round from behind her, and gripped on her arms. And she still looked away with that look like a smile. She shook like she was cold" (CE, 498-99).

It is Edmund Wilson's feeling that *The Huntsmen Are Up In*

America, the novel which took up so much of Bishop's energies in the 1920's, failed to materialize because Bishop's plans for finishing it, which involved the hero's return from Europe to take his place in America, were at odds with his own instinctive rejection of the culture of the United States (*CE,* x-xi). This suggestion is reasonable, but more than an apt conclusion was needed to set the book aright.

The major fault of the unpublished novel is that it is misconceived. It is a strange conglomeration of realistic prose and fantasy. Unlike "Porphirio" in that it deals with the present rather than with a Renaissance never-never land, the novel as it stands gives no indication that Bishop had any firm notion of how to fuse the worlds of romance and naturalism, of how to construct a novel on the order of Fitzgerald's *The Great Gatsby* or of Wilder's *The Cabala*—two contemporaneous works which Bishop's novel in some respects resembles. Novels with a high degree of the fantastic and bizarre were not uncommon during the years after World War I, and Bishop's novel suggests that he might have been adversely influenced by two of the most celebrated practitioners of romance, James Branch Cabell (there seem to be echoes of *The Rivet in Grandfather's Neck* in Bishop's novel) and Ronald Firbank's American disciple, Carl Van Vechten (the New York sections of *The Huntsmen Are Up In America* are more than vaguely reminiscent of Van Vechten's *The Blind Bow-Boy*).

The name which Bishop gives his hero, Brakespeare More-O'Brien, succinctly indicates the unrealistic dimensions of the book. Brakespeare is the son of a Virginia lady and an Irishman who began his life in America as a tavern fighter and racetrack adventurer. When the mother elopes with a visiting Englishman, the father turns his son over to his maternal grandfather. Brakespeare, growing up in an exclusively male household, receives his education in a scattered fashion from the grandfather, a relic of the eighteenth century who devotes most of his time to attempts to unravel his family history. Brakespeare only learns about women when he comes upon a painting of a Venetian courtesan whose favors one of his ancestors had enjoyed and when his uncle permits him to read an account of the courtesan's life (Wilson prints this chapter in the *Collected Essays*). He is so moved by the portrait that he writes a sonnet (the poem appears in *Minute Particulars* as "A Recollection") and decides to become a poet. His grandfather then sends him off to Venice, to learn something of life and perhaps to cure him of his itch to write. In Venice, Brakespeare falls in love with echoes of the past and quite joyously loses his virginity to a young prostitute.

When Brakespeare returns to America, the novel loses a good deal of momentum. Brakespeare's father has become enormously rich as a munitions maker, and the young repatriate lands in New York determined to lead the life of a modern "prince." He thinks that New York might prove to be a twentieth-century Venice, feeling that "now, however else it might fail, New York was intensely and variously alive." Bishop must have wanted very much to convert New York into a modern Venice; as the novel tails off, however, Brakespeare discovers it to be not much more than a nervous wasteland. He takes up with a New Englander he had met in Venice, a New Englander who has given himself over to composing jazz. Through him he meets an emancipated young American woman who can become sexually excited only after she has watched Negroes dance in Harlem. The unfinished novel ends, after a wild night in Harlem, with Brakespeare looking down upon the vacant and dawn-deserted streets of New York.

The Huntsmen Are Up In America is much too disjointed and rambling; it is weak because of the unrealized character of Brakespeare; and it is finally deficient because Bishop is not able to give direction and coherent meaning to the romance form which he utilizes. But the novel does exhibit his prose style at its most brilliant, and it also illuminates and points up several themes of great significance in Bishop's poetry and in his later fiction.

Brakespeare's grandfather had begun his historical researches "in a spirit of malice"—in the desire to confute his elders who, shortly after the Civil War, had begun to imagine "the life of the South before the war to have been courtly and abundant." As he burrows into the past, he comes to realize that there were further possibilities in his work, that it might "be made into a record relatively complete of the introduction, survival, change and decay of civilization in the United States." He recognizes that the proper end of his task is the presentation of "the essential humanity of his subject and the sensitiveness of his surface to

the luminous atmosphere in which he lived, to offer his person-
nages [sic] as men and yet at the same time to show them as
mirrors of an age."

As his imagination is more and more gripped by the task which
he has set himself, the grandfather concludes that the culture of
the South was imperfect but that it was a culture of men, men
who sincerely believed in the ideals which they set up for themselves. A man with a decided streak of Puritanism, he even comes
to accept the ancestor who had brought the portrait of the
courtesan to Virginia; he realizes that "a man can justify himself
as well on a lusty bed as in the library of the noblest platonist.
There he is as pretentious as anywhere and, in spite of all
appearance, no more naked. For it is in our animal nature that
we differ most from the other animals, and it is no accident
that it is so."

The Huntsmen Are Up In America clearly reveals that Bishop
had rejected the New England ideal long before he wrote "The
Missing All." He embodies his criticism of New England largely
in his portraits of the jazz composer, Cotton Abbot, and the
modern American woman, Virginia Hamish. Bishop also gives a
good deal of space to Brakespeare's grandfather's account of his
own father, a Southerner who had embraced the doctrines of
Emerson and other Transcendentalists. Abbot, as his name suggests, is sexless and colorless. Unable to find any sustenance in
the tradition of his forebears, he fails to appreciate the richness
of Venice which so captivates Brakespeare. Later on he gives
himself over to Negro jazz, which in the New York portions of
the novel is depicted as alien and destructive to the whites who
abandon themselves to its primitive insistence.

In like fashion, Virginia Hamish, in spite of the freedom which
she enjoys as a modern American woman, is totally unlike the
two Venetian prostitutes who reveal the wonders of sex to Brakespeare. Frustrated and without passion, except when she is
spurred to hysterical sexuality by watching the wild dancing of
Negro women, she is one of Henry Adams' American virgins,
robbed of her femininity by the forces of the dynamo. The novel
suggests that both she and Abbot are as much victims of the
aberrations of New England culture as was Brakespeare's great-
grandfather, who neglected the duties of his estate to moon away
his days in Transcendentalist reveries.

Brakespeare's grandfather places the blame for his father's dereliction at the door of the seductive Ralph Waldo Emerson, and Bishop's novel contains a portrait of Emerson that sets the key for the thunderous battery of attacks which Southern writers fired against the sage of Concord during the late 1920's and 1930's: "A shrewd and decorous mystic, with sad side-whiskers, vainly trying to contemplate his umbilicus through a boiled shirt and a broadcloth waistcoat. Vainly because he could not keep from straying to some little concern of the yankee world about him.... That was the trouble with them all, even Thoreau, the most vigorous, racy and imaginative of the lot; they were hideously provincial."

Bishop's novel, while deeming the culture of the South imperfect and rejecting New England culture as noxious to the human spirit, does set up one society as an ideal—Venice at the height of its power. When Brakespeare visits Venice, he sees it as a city which, for a short while at least, was able to resolve the conflicting demands of "force" and "form." It was a city which enabled man to realize his animal needs while giving order to those needs, a city which managed to provide a satisfactory outlet for man's aspirations and illusions, a city which, above all, permitted its artists to live up to what Brakespeare considers is the poet's primary responsibility: "to live in his own age, and not merely to breathe its air, but to stand at its very front and furthest confine." When Brakespeare returns home after his journey to Venice and his grandfather asks him if he has decided what he should like to be in life, he replies, "Sir? O, another Venice." His grandfather snorts at his reply, but Brakespeare goes on: "I mean ... that I should like to have a mind which, so far as it is possible for a mind, should have that power which the Venetian State at its height surely had—to serenely admit all contradictions, to splendidly reconcile all opposites." He concludes his praise of Venice by invoking the figure of speech central to Bishop's poem, "Speaking of Poetry": "it was only there, I am sure, that the ceremony could have been found that would wed Desdemona to her black Moor."

For Brakespeare, as well as for Bishop, Venice was a city where art and ritual could give shape to the forces that were always threatening to explode into chaos. Against the foil of the Venetian ideal, Bishop sets three forms of American society. The New England ideal is unsatisfactory because it refuses to admit the existence of forces inimical to man and because it has attempted to do away with tradition. New York, the modern city, is an expression of force, but New York cannot control the energies which it concentrates; its shape is monstrous rather than artistic. The culture of the South is admirable in that it recognizes human frailties and has a respect for tradition and ritual; Southern society, however, is decaying and moribund, and its traditions have been adulterated by sentimentality. More importantly, the South is culturally feeble because it does not possess a vital artistic heritage. It is not irrelevant that Brakespeare's grandfather keeps the portrait of Alessandrina hidden and that he is unable to respond to his grandson's enthusiasm for Venice.

In the years after he had put aside *The Huntsmen Are Up In America,* Bishop frequently turned in his essays, fiction, and poetry to the evaluation of various forces within American culture. Never afterward, though, did he attempt in fiction to juggle and contrast several of them as he did in his unpublished novel. Perhaps he had learned from his unsuccessful effort that such an encompassing view was beyond his powers, and perhaps this recognition of his limitations helped to focus and order his later fiction. And yet, it is to be regretted that Bishop did limit himself; for *The Huntsmen Are Up In America,* in spite of its failure as a novel, markedly demonstrates that Bishop had a firm grasp upon the conflicts and tensions within American society. If he had started anew upon a novel of wide sweep and dimensions, perhaps he would have been able to give it some of that gravity-defying form which he admired in Venetian art and which is so conspicuously lacking in *The Huntsmen Are Up In America.*

II   *The Mordington Cycle*

Many Thousands Gone, which appeared in 1931 and which takes its title from Bishop's prize-winning short story published in *Scribner's Magazine,* contains his best short fiction and is on many counts superior to the novel he published several years afterward. Because all five of the stories take place in and about the Shenandoah town of Mordington and because there is a linear projection of time in the stories—the action of the first occurring prior to the Civil War and that of the last extending up to the turn of the century—it is tempting to view them as an organic whole, on the order, say, of *Winesburg, Ohio* or *Go Down,*

Moses. Cecil D. Elby, the only critic who has discussed Bishop's fiction at any length, takes just such an approach in his article, "The Fiction of John Peale Bishop."

Elby argues that Bishop's fiction is motivated by a rejection of the myth of the Old South and by his feeling that the eighteenth-century tradition in Virginia, already in decay prior to the Civil War, was hopelessly disintegrated by the end of the nineteenth century. In Elby's view, Bishop's volume of stories depicts a "South that was sterile and decadent long before the Confederacy existed"; the fictional town of Mordington "evokes associations of death and is for Bishop the microcosm of the modern South."[6]

Elby's thesis, while not altogether unsound, suffers from his reluctance to examine what Bishop has actually said about the South. He fails also to perceive the ironies and ambiguities playing throughout the stories, and his argument is rendered doubly shaky by the fact that the time scheme of the stories and their common locale are not enough to provide them with the sort of thematic unity that Elby would like to see in them. The stories are not, to be sure, totally unrelated; they share a consistent tone and they are all, in one way or another, about the South and its history. They do not, however, reject the traditions of the South as utterly as Elby believes.

Even more importantly, it is unwise to view the stories merely as allegories setting forth Bishop's view of Southern history. All five of them, in varying degrees, assess and judge the Southern tradition; but the "myths" with which they deal are more various and more universal than the myth of the Old South. Mordington does evoke "associations of death," but Shenandoah Valley towns have no monopoly on death. The Mordington of Bishop's fiction is both unique and like any other town: a place where death is always lurking and where there is always the possibility of love— and also the possibility that love, distorted and perverted, may itself prove to be a form of death. If *Many Thousands Gone* has a central theme, that theme is the one of Bishop's mature work: man is mortal and his humanity precarious.

The first story in the collection, "The Corpse in the House," set in the decade prior to the outbreak of the Civil War, focuses upon a young lawyer-politician's discovery that he is no longer in love with the girl to whom he has been affianced for several years. The girl has delayed marriage in order to stay on as companion to her aged grandmother; after the death of the old woman George Cochrane awakens to find that he no longer loves Rose Doyne. When Cochrane, after receiving the news of the death, waits for Rose in the old woman's old-fashioned parlor, he remembers her as "an old horror" but also grudgingly admits that she had been an imperious personage. He also realizes that not merely the gap between their ages separates Mrs. Doyne from her granddaughter. Rose is mild and gentle, a perfect specimen of nineteenth-century gentility; "Mrs. Doyne belonged to another day and kept its manners—crude and punctilious. She scratched when she felt like it, she swore at Eliza, and to the end of her eighty years refused to wear underdrawers." It was her habit to insist, "'I'm a lady, I was brought up to petticoats.'" And Cochrane has to admit that, in her own fashion, she was a lady: "She was born under George III and she knew how to be high and mighty."

Cochrane is aware of her presence in the parlor with its faded mythological wallpaper, and he, lounging in her wingchair, remembers how she sat, even in her decrepitude: "She would have sat in stiffer state, a cushion behind her, not to lean on, but to keep her upright; she talked in a mobcap, her great nose like a hacked blade." He remembers particularly one day when he had stood in front of her fire and the old lady, to "poor Rose's confusion," had cackled: "'Rose, I see you've caught a Virginian. . . . I can always tell Virginians—I can tell 'em by their cold arses.'"[7]

Outside the curtained windows, spring is just beginning to touch the landscape, but when Rose comes into the parlor and permits Cochrane to embrace her, he has the feeling that "Her hair had the smell of dead leaves" (11). After going upstairs with Rose to view the corpse, Cochrane is upset to notice how young Mrs. Doyne seems; he can mouth only sententious platitudes. Looking at the corpse, he remembers the eight years he has waited, that he had asked Rose to marry him "on a day like this, sunny with wind, but in another April." When Rose, looking across the bed at him, suddenly asks, "'You'll forgive me?,'" Cochrane is unable to respond immediately. Finally, however, "touched by her request as though she had been a timid child," (14-17), he gives her his promise and the two go to inspect the newly dug grave.

In the family burying ground, where the marble slabs are obscured by long grass, Cochrane remembers that Rose had led him here when he first called on her:

> She had brought him then as now among the tombs, pointing out names, pausing to read the disconsolate verses. She put up her hands to sniff the bitter box and her slender arms had charmed him. She knelt above the little mounds, where mouldy lambs and broken cherub heads in stone perpetuated childish innocence. She wept over each of these lost children, Adelaide and little Georgie and Ann Lucy, dead all of them long before she was born. Such melancholy was adorable. When they came out again, her eyes were all dewy and dark. Having seen her in tears, he found he loved her. (25)

Observing Rose among the graves, now "sallow and peaked, . . . wrapped in black against the wind, silent, in an old bonnet with bedraggled strings," he knows suddenly that he loves her no longer. He also perceives that he cannot step aside from the future that now awaits him: "There would be a decent period of mourning, with Rose in black. And afterwards they would be married. That also he knew" (26).

The new grave into which Cochrane and Rose stare symbolizes the death of their love, a love even more frustrated and thwarted than the brief lives of the "lost children" mouldering among the boxwood. Out of a misplaced sense of duty and a misplaced tenderness, Rose and Cochrane have put off the fulfillment of their love until its fruition is no longer possible. In their case, such procrastination was more than unwise; for the foundations of love were precarious to begin with. Rose is a not-too-distant relative of Mark Twain's Emmeline Grangerford; Cochrane had initially become enamored of Rose because of her fragility and her "adorable melancholy." The "corpse in the house" of their love has not been old Mrs. Doyne so much as their own fatuity. The story is, to a certain extent, a commentary on the gulf between the urgent vitality of the eighteenth century and the sentimentality and sententiousness of the nineteenth, but it is something more than a cultural parable: it is a story of misplaced and missed love.

The next three stories in *Many Thousands Gone* take place during the Civil War. The first of these, "The Cellar," which Fitzgerald thought the best of the lot, is narrated by a Confederate veteran long after the close of the war. The story is not an account of military exploits but of an atrocity perpetrated by a civilian. The old veteran does not hold with the latter-day notion that soldiers are brutalized by their experiences, but he does believe that civilians sucked into the maelstrom of war can behave savagely; he tells the story of Charlie Ambler to demonstrate his point.

Ambler is one of three brothers who live on a farm outside Mordington. With the onset of war, his elder and younger brothers enter the Confederate army, but Charlie hires a replacement and stays at home to take care of the farm and his mother. Charlie is awkward and lumpish; and his mother, a dominating and garrulous woman who much resembles Mrs. Doyne, constantly berates and belittles him. Early in the war, Mrs. Ambler is an enthusiastic supporter of the Confederate cause; later on, after her youngest son is reported missing, she becomes dispirited and apathetic, and eventually she dies. During the summer of Gettysburg, Charlie slumps into idleness and lets the few Negroes remaining on his place look after the crops. He takes to wearing cast-off uniform trousers and an army revolver on his hip, and he spends most of his time drinking and watching card games in back rooms of Mordington.

One day, he rides home to discover that looters from the Federal army have strayed to his place and, under the impression that they have discovered a hiding place for treasure, have rooted up his mother's grave and spilled her corpse out of its wooden coffin. When Charlie comes upon the scene, warned by a small Negro boy who tells him there are six men in the party, all the looters are in the cellar beneath the house. Barricading all but one entrance to the cellar, Charlie slaughters five of the men as they attempt escape into the upper air. He waits out the night, and next morning desperately enters the cellar; he finds no one left alive, however, and concludes that the boy was either mistaken or that one man had taken his booty and left before his arrival.

Afterward, Charlie frequently boasts of his deed. As the narrator puts it, Charlie talks as "if he were relating some horrible thing that had happened in battle.... Yes, I think Ambler looked on himself—after the war—as a soldier." When the man who has been listening to the tale remonstrates, "But, after all, he was defending his own soil," the old soldier admits that such a case might be made out for Charlie; he concludes the story, however, by remarking: "But I don't think you can really. It's not as if he'd been a soldier—it's not at all as if he'd been a soldier" (105).

Elby argues that Charlie's actions should be interpreted as a gesture directed against the stultifying Southern code: "By his violent act Charlie breaks through the code and becomes at last a human being with a will of his own. Yet the murder of these soldiers, which would have been commendable upon the battlefield, becomes the stigmata of his disgrace among other Virginians. Both within and without the ring of tradition he finds only rejection."[8] There is very little merit in such an argument. The story in no way derides the military code for which the veteran is a spokesman; and there is no reason to assume that the significance of the old soldier's tale is to be arrived at only by turning what he has to say upside down. Charlie Ambler does not become "a human being with a will of his own" when he murders the five men of the looting party; he becomes a butcher, and the story is simply an account of his brutalization. "The Cellar" is not a simple story, however, and Bishop's account of the slaying of the five men is masterful. The violence is beautifully controlled, and Bishop's restrained prose is played off against the mayhem which it so incisively captures. It is very likely that the story owes something to Hemingway's accounts of warfare and slaughter, but Bishop has succeeded in making his prose something more than an imitation of Hemingway. The following paragraph, which describes what happens when the fourth soldier leaves the cellar, is a good index of Bishop's stylistic accomplishment:

> He had grown cramped and the first rain had begun to fall, large drops that spotted the ground, when the door swung open with a bang, and a young Yankee stood there, surprised that the door had yielded so easily. That was all—his expression hardly changed when Charlie's bullets took him in the belly. He fell over backward, loosening the pole he held under his arm. The door swung empty on the dark entrance. (99-100)

There is a "corpse in the house" of the third story of the collection, but "Young Death and Desire" does not deal with the denial and starvation of love. In this story, death is not the sign of love's decay; it is, rather, the force which prompts love's fruition.

"Young Death and Desire" is told from the point of view of the daughter of one of Mordington's doctors. The town has been turned into a hospital and morgue after one of the Civil War battles, and there are three soldiers in the cellar-kitchen of her house. Two die from their wounds soon after her father carries them in, and the third is dying from a ragged hole in his throat. At nightfall, when a corporal arrives to take the three soldiers away to be buried, Cecily is horrified to discover that he intends to take all three. To her shocked protests, the corporal replies, " 'I got to get on. I'm sorry for him. He'll be dead by the time we get to the graveyard.' " She continues to argue with him, and even though he insists—" 'Listen! I can't help being hard. I've seen too many like him in the last few days. Besides, it's me next time' " (118-19)—he finally sends his burial detail away into the darkness. While Cecily gives the corporal something to eat and a drink from her father's sideboard, she talks with him about the war. She gathers little from his offhand way of speaking; he talks of battles as if "they were hills and woods and streams he had seen." Cecily, however, knows "that when he was old he could still say Malvern and Gaines' Mill, Seven Pines and the second Bull Run—I was young and I was there. And as she looked at him in the candlelight he seemed to live in a lustre as of bronze" (122). Cecily finally persuades the corporal to wash and go to sleep in her bed; and, after her father comes home and goes upstairs, she settles down to watch over the dying soldier.

After Cecily's candle gutters out while she is keeping watch, she recites childhood charm-rhymes to keep at bay the shadows in the dark kitchen. Suddenly, she realizes that blood is pouring from the soldier's bandages. She runs to awaken the corporal, who is "naked in the white bed," and he sleepily embraces her as Cecily sinks "unresisting into the drowsy warmth of his embrace." Then she springs back and tells him the wounded soldier is dying. Waiting in the parlor while he pulls on his clothes, she finds that she is "cold all over," her hands trembling and her teeth chattering (130-31). At the corporal's direction, she hurries to the sideboard to get a drink for the soldier; but, when she returns, she finds him dead in the corporal's arms. In response to her urging, the corporal carries the corpse outside. When he returns, Cecily immediately senses that the corporal is

aflame with sexual desire, and she puts up no resistance when he
hungrily makes love to her:

> His arms were around her, hard and alive. Her least resistance
> set on his desire. They met, they merged, they were lost in a
> furious folly. Her mouth sought his, and her life was drawn out,
> like copper wire in a flame.
>
> "Please," the voice was hoarse that pled. She was all weakness
> and could not answer. He laid her head down.
>
> She had nothing with which not to yield and let the darkness
> close round her, soft, warm and profound; in the dark her breath
> came in long shuffling sighs on the throat of her lover.... She
> could not stay his invading violence.
>
> The black of the kitchen was enormous. On the table the
> candle stood with bright thrusting flame. It dribbled wax, down
> the sides; with a sputter of the wick, the hot fluid overflowed,
> congealed in sputtering drops. The wax had the shape of
> tears. (135-36)

The symbolism of the final paragraph is perhaps a bit too
flamboyant; the description of their sexual encounter, however,
well conveys the urgency of the desires which engulf the girl
and the young soldier. Then, after the corporal grows sleepy
and boyishly embarrassed in Cecily's arms, the prose slows
down to reflect her bemused wonder and her slow recognition
of what she has done. Cecily has felt pain, but has been assured
of her own vitality. She has given herself to life; and, though
she is not fully aware of it, her living pain has been an answer
to the grim cargo which a loutish wagoner had driven up to her
house early the previous morning: "Soldiers had been piled in
his wagon as deep as another; the straw of the bed was drenched.
Blood had spattered the spokes of the hind wheels, the back-
board was like the sides of a henhouse where chickens are killed
on the block" (111).

Cecily knows full well that she will come to regret what she
has done, but she spurns regret while she holds her lover in her
arms. She is joyous in her possession of life, and the concluding
words of the story make it quite clear that she has come to life
because, for a short while at least, she has been able to set at
bay the inevitability of death. She has accepted her place in
nature, and for a moment has been able to rise above death—
by yielding to life's fierce imperatives: "In the window she was
aware of a faint light; morning was near. But still for a little

while she could hold this happiness, hold it against the very
turning of the earth that turned them toward the sun. They were
not dead" (137).

"Many Thousands Gone," the last of the Civil War stories, is
not, as the title might suggest, a tale of runaway slaves. Slaves
figure largely in the story, but only as representative elements
of the society of wartime Mordington. And "Many Thousands
Gone" is not so much a tightly knit story as a series of loosely
related sketches detailing the behavior of Mordington's citizens
and of the invading troops when the town is occupied for a day
and a night by a Federal force moving down the Shenandoah
Valley. Although the various episodes never coalesce to form a
single story line, Bishop does impart a certain unity to the
sketches. The shifting point of view remains observantly neutral,
and the style throughout is reserved and chary of figurative
language. Bishop also provides a degree of coherence by inter-
weaving his selected personages through different episodes; furthermore, most of the sketches are unified by their disclosure of
what happens to people when the ordinary bonds of discipline
and routine are loosened. And, finally, the various episodes
achieve a certain unity as, gathering momentum, they hurry
toward the several acts of violence, two of them involving death,
which cluster near the end of the story.

Because the story is so long (it makes up more than one-third
of the volume) and because its various strands are after all only
tenuously related, it would be wasteful of time and space to
discuss all its parts at length. One may say, though, that the story
is of a piece with most of Bishop's other fiction in its concentration on violence and death. The story also resembles the others
in the volume in its portrait of the disorder and needless waste
that have irrupted into the life of the South. It is this aspect of
the story that perhaps needs the most attention, particularly
since Elby has argued that Bishop, "having weighed the im-
perfections and limitations of the Virginia tradition,... now
destroys it utterly as he shows Mordington helpless and vanquished by the hated Yankees." In Elby's view, "The rape of
Mordington symbolizes the ultimate desecration of the South as
both country and culture and ends forever its claim to moral
and political superiority."[9] Although it is difficult to see how a
rape destroys whatever claims the victim might advance, Elby's
argument may be countered on more than rhetorical grounds.

While all the various strands of the story have something to say about the South and its violation by the North, there are two particular episode-sequences which most fully dramatize Bishop's conflicting attitudes toward the South. One sequence describes the bewilderment and confusion of a spinster daughter of a deceased West Pointer when she discovers that her pretensions to gentility count for nothing with the invaders. Shunted aside when she goes to army headquarters to obtain a guard for herself and her invalid sister, she suffers the indignity of being kissed on the street by a young infantryman; later, her genteel protests are ineffectual when a search party ransacks her home. Faced with the shame and horrors of the present, Miss Cary, who has imagined herself to be "the very type of young Southern womanhood" (155), can do nothing but revert to the past. Remembering the days when her mother and father had been alive, she thinks: "O, but life had been lovely then!" Finally, unable to look at the disarray which the soldiers have left in the house, she goes out into the night and gives herself over to what is unmistakably a death wish: "On her face she felt the rain and then her loose hair misted with rain. O sweet it was to the breath and on her face cool and clean! There could not be enough of it. She wished she could feel it run through her, as it ran through the bones of the dead." She recalls all the young men who have perished in the war and suddenly realizes she is no longer young and will never marry: "There were so many that the rain fell on that night, so many that were dead. It makes me feel so old, she said, everyone I know is dead" (213-15).

Miss Cary, then, may be viewed as a figure symbolizing the impotence and decay of the old traditions of the South, but Bishop does not end on the note of her dismay. The story concludes with the return to life of her sister, long bedfast in her illness, who rises up in fury when soldiers invade her room and pull her from her bed. She thunders Old Testament curses at the soldiers, and when Miss Cary comes into her room on the morning when the troops are pulling out of town, she discovers Sister Hester up and about. Miss Cary has suffered a spiritual death, but Hester, also a Southern lady, has been shocked into new life. The last words of the story are hers, and while they function as ironically as the title of "Resurrection," the biblical message which she crazily misquotes has a double-edged ambiguity: "I am the Resurrection and the Death!" (239). In Hester's case, as in Cecily Burwell's, new life and death go hand in hand.

The other story-line of "Many Thousands Gone" of prime importance as an expression of Bishop's feelings about the South deals with the actions of the Union commander. Colonel Strother happens to be a native of Mordington, but he is consumed with hatred for all Virginians. Strother is under orders to bring the war home to the civilian population of the South, but the action he takes to reveal "*the hard hand of war*" (152) to the people of Mordington is unique: he burns down the house in which he was born and in which he has spent much of his childhood.

Strother's bitterness results partly from his realization that his mother had returned to her parents' home for his birth in order to avoid scandal in the Northern town where she had gone to live with her husband, that he was "what they call down here the engagement child"; but Strother insists to himself that his resentment does not arise altogether from the circumstances of his birth and childhood. As he gazes out the window "through which as a boy of eleven he had stared at the snow and the black shadows of the winter moon" and sees his soldiers preparing a bonfire of hay and polished furniture, he tells himself: "I don't know why I hate them. Damn 'em, I just do. I despise the ground they walk on." Watching the first flames dance in the piled hay, just before he himself sets fire to hay strewn about the carpet of his aunt's parlor, he goes on with his monologue of self-justification: "I just don't like them. I don't like their manners, I don't like their ways.... I despise the ground they walk on.... They are all alike—shiftless and pretentious. Virginians!... And to think, by God, I was born one——" (177-78).

Allen Tate has suggested that the description of Colonel Strother (a man with "small shiny uncertain eyes" that seem to shorten his "sharp nose" and increase "the already extraordinary foxlike quality of his features") contains "a caricature of Bishop himself" (*CP*, xii). If this is true, the emphasis must be placed on the word "caricature"; it seems unwise to assume, as Elby does, that Bishop shares Strother's sentiments. Strother's vengeful act in no way establishes him as a man superior to the Virginians whom he despises; the flames which consume his birthplace merely set in relief his own barbarism. At bottom, Strother's gesture is an act of self-destruction, and his purposeless fury is a sign of his inner emptiness. Strother is able to set fire to the house which embodies the Virginia tradition, but he offers no substitute for the tradition which he so bitterly rejects. By no means an apology for the Old South and its curious code, "Many Thousands Gone" certainly suggests that the shapeless, brutal culture which overwhelmed it—that culture which Colonel Strother has embraced in his flight from Virginia—can hardly claim to be superior to that of the vanquished South.

The fifth and final story in *Many Thousands Gone* is quite unlike the stories which precede it. The first four stories are all realistic narratives; "If Only," however, is patently a fantasy, and for once Bishop succeeds completely in giving point and direction to his aristocratic impulses toward romance. In large measure, his success results from his strategy of using naturalistic details and a prose style as down to earth as that employed in the four other stories; but it also comes from his having hit on a fable powerful enough to carry the burden of his tale, which utilizes the playful world of fantasy to comment on what we generally take to be the realm of fact.

As in the first and third stories of the collection, there is a "corpse in the house" of "If Only." In this case, though, the corpse appears in the guise of a man of flesh and blood: a Negro cook and serving-man who looks after the spinster Sabine sisters. The sisters take up residence in Mordington after the close of the Civil War, and for the first couple of years they undergo a succession of shiftless servants. One summer morning, after they have prostrated themselves cleaning up the litter left behind by a departed cook, one of the sisters discovers Bones deftly peeling potatoes in their kitchen. He smilingly introduces himself, and informs Lou that he has come to work for her and her sister Ellen. Although the sisters are a bit taken aback by his unheralded appearance, Bones is the very image of respectability, even aristocracy; and they are immediately impressed by his genteel manner. In the days to come, Bones only heightens the sisters' "impression that here was a godsend.... He mentioned names, the oldest and the best, but it was his manners that proved him. In the kitchen he was easy and polite, grand in the dining room" (*MTG*, 258). Bones is a superlative housekeeper, but it is his culinary skill that most amazes them: "Under his long bony fingers all the savors of the old South revived in their kitchen."

Unfortunately, the Sabines are not accustomed to such fare,

and "they frequently lay awake half the night forgetting Bones' suppers." They dare not complain, though, and proudly recall that "Jefferson Davis had also been a sufferer from dyspepsia" (259-60). Extravagant in his marketing, Bones also expects high wages; the sisters conclude, however, that "He was really a marvel—so clean, so temperate! Moreover, he was an Episcopalian. They could ask for nothing more." So, in spite of their occasional misgivings about the costs of Bones's upkeep, and in spite of their nervousness when they realize that their servant seems never to sleep, the Sabine sisters agree that "Bones was worth it. They had lived so long in a dream that it was sweet to taste the reality. With this one tall, black, jovial Negro in the house it was as though the war had never been or, having been fought, had turned to a triumph for the South. The old molds were restored. It was indeed as though dead bones were alive again" (261-62).

Time passes, even though Bishop in his role of narrator makes it clear that the Sabine sisters attempt to live outside of time: "They did not withstand time, they denied it. And nothing changed. . . . They held out against time, and were aware only of time's sensuous coloring, which we know as weather" (265, 267). Then one winter Sunday, when she has stayed home from church, Lou comes upon Bones in their bathroom. He is standing naked in the tub, standing "terrible and tall, . . . and very black," and he is flicking a wet towel against his "bright black body." Bones chuckles and winks at her, but he does not stop his game. She escapes from the bathroom and waits until she can share her "terror and confusion" with her sister. They are sitting huddled in the parlor when Bones appears and announces dinner, "an impeccable reflection, in white jacket and black trousers" (268). He goes about his work unabashed, and the two sisters find themselves unable to speak to him. His cooking is still as good as ever, and the dinner that follows is so calmly and excellently served that their terror seems out of place. After talking among themselves, and even after Lou persuades Ellen that she really did see Bones naked in the tub, they decide to remain silent about the incident in the bathroom.

Bones now becomes "grander than ever." When the time for spring cleaning comes, he does over the whole house, giving their downstairs rooms a polished and spare elegance which has an "air and discomfort that was almost colonial." Bones's nocturnal prowlings set them on edge, however, and they agree that "A thing that slept so little could hardly be a man" (274). Finally, one summer afternoon when Ellen discovers the Negro asleep on her bed, the sisters summon Lou's aging suitor, Mr. Hite, who does manage to dismiss the servant. Bones departs, tears in his eyes, but that same night they hear his banjo tinkling in the back-corridor bedroom. All night long they hear him singing and playing, and next morning he calmly serves breakfast. After announcing that he is going to commence a boxwood maze, he leaves them alone with their coffee.

The sisters now realize their servant is back to stay, and now they blandly confront the terror they will know with Bones in the house—telling each other that since "he had been their intimate so long, they could not reasonably confine him to a lunatic cell. They would feel themselves mad." After looking their future squarely in the face, the Sabine sisters feel something of relief; they take comfort in the realization that Bones will prove to be a source of gratification as well as fright: "They knew now what they owed him. With him they lived in terror, but in the tradition. Their digestions were destroyed, their nerves frayed, but their pride sustained" (280-81).

At first glance, "If Only" seems to be a rather obvious parable which demonstrates the palpable defects of that "tradition" to which the Sabines are bound—a story which supports Elby's conclusion that Bishop's fiction rests on the conviction that "A return to the past would yield only the burial rites of a civilization long dead."[10] It is true that the two sisters are guilty of a foolish and futile effort to live outside of time, and it is also true that they attempt to escape from life rather than to immerse themselves in it. Lou, particularly, has denied life by permitting her youth to slip away as she and her suitor continue their never-consummated courtship. Of their unending romance, Bishop remarks: "There was always the same trembling anticipation of delight, never a conclusion. She was still the young girl to be adored and pursued but not touched, he the lover who worshipping sought and never came to hard and male possession" (266). As Lou grows older, the General Lee whom she so much reveres comes to haunt her nightmares, and one might well say that Bones is a visitation upon her for her denial of love as well as a visitation upon her and her sister for their denial of the present and retreat to the past. Bones *is* the past, the "good nigger" of the ante-bellum South, and his horror is compounded by the fact that he, the Negro, is the repository and carrier of all the refinements and graces of the Southern past. Bones is also Death (as well as the Negro skeleton in the conscience of the South), and one would hardly wish to set aside the story's suggestion that the end of the ante-bellum tradition, as the Sabine sisters live it, is death.

To stop at this point, however, is to miss the full impact of the story. Bones is Death, but he also brings vitality and a certain fulfillment to the lives of the two maiden sisters. As Bishop says, with him they live in terror, but they live also within the satisfying illusions of a tradition. While that tradition might be uncomfortable, it is not without grandeur. And even though their nerves are shot and they suffer dyspepsia, the Sabines manage to retain their pride. Furthermore, within the story, Bones becomes an embodiment of all those forces which threaten to destroy life but which, in Bishop's view, can be ordered to a certain extent if their existence is but admitted. In many ways, the Sabine sisters war against reality, but they do accept Bones; by doing so, they draw from him some of his terror and make him their support.

In a passage near the close of the story, a passage which also makes explicit his own love for the land of his birth, Bishop clearly indicates Bones's symbolic value for the two women whom he takes captive:

> They were like that Valley in which they had been born and which they loved and which indeed, as it lies between two ridges of intensely blue hills, is a country to be loved. The richness of its soil it owes to a slow disintegration; water has worn its rocks as noiselessly as time and all underneath the dark is hollow. The Sabines were slowly decomposing, like the limestone which arched and caverned underlies the long Valley and worried by water minutely decays. With Bones gone, they felt the hollowness underground (281).

Bones, even though he is Death, perhaps because he is Death, is their prop against their own disintegration. With all its faults, and with all its horrors, the tradition to which the Sabine sisters give allegiance is able to bring order into their lives. The price they pay is a terrible one, but perhaps it is not excessive. Bones is, as the last words of the story make clear, "as it were a dear obsession," one which the Sabines will keep "till they were dead" (282). One should note, however, that the adjective modifying "obsession" has at least two relevant connotations: it can be taken to mean high in cost, but it also means worthy of love.[11] Bishop's attitude toward the South was not a simple one, and "If Only" is a fine, fully realized story which tantalizingly sets forth that mixture of undeniable love for, and withdrawal from, their homeland that has characterized so many twentieth-century writers of the South.

III   *Coming of Age in Mordington*

Near the close of Bishop's single published novel, *Act of Darkness* (1935), the young first-person narrator, after shaking off a self-imposed illness that has brought him near death, turns to reading poetry as one means of gratifying "those appetites which [he] had suppressed almost at the cost of [his] life." Poetry is not foreign to him, but in the past he has preferred the poetry of the nineteenth century, that of Shelley in particular; now for the first time he comes upon *Othello*. As he fascinatedly reads the tragedy, he makes a significant discovery:

> This was poetry and in it my life was renewed. All those passions which had perplexed me so I sickened, here in the verse were pitched to their utmost intensity. But it was possible to share them and stand aloof from their conclusion. I could be compelled by the Pontic sea of Othello's rage, swept in the flood, play in the tumultuous swell, be lifted to the last on its rising surge and not, when it broke, tumbled, fell, go under and be dragged backward in its retiring ebb. I could be, and not be overcome.[12]

Some time afterward, just as young John is getting ready to leave Mordington to attend school in the North, he reads the play once more. This second reading fails to provide him with the same "conscious escape from time, a seeing beyond space" (359), but he now realizes why he had been so moved by the tragedy and begins to perceive the full measure of Shakespeare's mastery.

John notes that his sympathy with the play's characters and his "contemplation of their passions in action had so illumined [his] mind that the people by whom [he] was surrounded became real ... as they had not been before." After reading *Othello*, John finds he is able to forgive his uncle Charlie, the person in his own drama whose shame and debasement had caused him such anguish. John can forgive Charlie just as he came to forgive himself on the night when his illness reached its crisis, when, "very close to death," he had learned, "Every soul is irremediably itself." John remarks that he might have learned from other authors, particularly from the "wise old moralist of Ecclesiastes," to "contemplate the vanity of human actions, and to value them, not by their reward when done, but by what recompense they have while doing." He insists, however, that from Shakespeare alone could he "have learned to share commonest passions in full responsibility for their consequences."

In John's view, the serenity with which the reader is able to observe the passions of Desdemona and her Moor is not to be traced to the fact that *Othello* unfolds a tale old even when Shakespeare took it up: "But it was not because they were remote in time that I could, despite my pity, regard these unhappy events in inhuman calm. No. Rather it was because they had been removed from time. The poet had imposed a sensuous order on the moral disorder of the world, his own and the Venetian's." Looking back upon the actions in which he has been involved and remembering the debasement of his idol, Charlie, he knows that the tragedy of Othello and Desdemona differs from that which he has witnessed not "merely in that measured and enraptured speech which Shakespeare had invented for his actors," even though the verse, "having form, had made possible a continuous sensuous excitement." It is not the poetic diction which sets *Othello* apart, but its "poetic order." *Othello* discloses "a conscious harmony of discordant emotions, to which the verse constantly responded. And beyond the art, though manifest only in the art, since it was simultaneous with it, was a way of seeing the world, or, more accurately, of imagining its passions in action" (360-62).

These passages near the end of *Act of Darkness*—which echo many of Bishop's critical comments on verse and the function of form in poetry—are highly illuminating insofar as they celebrate that conscious artistry upon which he most depended as a means of ordering the destructive forces he saw impinging upon man. He believed that man could, by means of his powers as an artist, give at least the illusion of meaning to his life—and make that life not only bearable but magnificent. Unfortunately, however, Bishop's praise of Shakespeare's formal artistry, that artistry which was "simultaneous" with his "way of seeing the world," points up the fact that *Act of Darkness* does not achieve a thoroughly satisfactory wedding of humane vision and artistic form.

One minor but irritating defect of the novel is Bishop's cavalier handling of the point of view. The story is told by and seen through the eyes of young John (his surname is never given). It is essential that the story be related in such a fashion, for its primary emphasis is upon John's growing up and his delivery from the sickness which threatens to destroy him. Many of the events of the story, however, are beyond the ken of the first-person narrator. Bishop proceeds to relate them as if John had been an invisible witness, making no effort to vary the style and narrative tone in his reporting of those scenes from which his young narrator is necessarily absent.

A more serious defect results from the collapse of the novel into two disjointed parts. The first half deals, in rather diffuse fashion, with the death of John's father and with John's adolescent delights and misgivings. This section reports upon his relations with members of his family and with various citizens of Mordington, his boyhood reading, his companionship with other boys of the town, and the pangs and doubts attendant upon the first stirrings of his sexual urges. The second half focuses upon the "act of darkness" which gives the novel its title, and upon the consequences of that act: the denunciation of Charlie as a rapist, Charlie's trial and eventual imprisonment, and John's sickening after he has witnessed the shattering of the ideal he had imagined Charlie to be.

To a certain extent, these halves of the novel are not unrelated. In the first half, Bishop introduces most of the principals of the courtroom drama, and John's eventual illness is not unconnected with his earlier self-doubts and questioning fears about his manhood; ultimately, however, the first portion of the book fails to link up with the second half. Although the trial and shame of his uncle lead directly to John's illness, and are therefore bound up with his youthful fears and hopes, Charlie's trial is not consequent upon most of what goes on in the first half of the book. Charlie's trial is a public drama, but the opening half deals with the private world of John's adolescence. In the second half, until after the close of the trial, John's thoughts and actions are minimized. At the novel's close, Bishop attempts to link up the two parts, but large fragments of the varied material of the first part refuse to lend themselves to such a fusion—and contribute little to what becomes the dominant concern of the book. Fitzgerald found fault with the structure of the book on just these grounds when he wrote to Bishop after its publication: "The first half of your book is so heavy with stimuli and promises, that the latter catastrophe of the rape is minimized—both in itself and in its consequences."[13]

It seems fairly obvious that in the first portion of the novel Bishop was attempting to accomplish two separate ends, ends not necessarily in conflict but ones which he did not attain with equal success and which he was not able to weld into a coherent whole. Bishop succeeds admirably in conveying the joys and terrors of John's adolescence—his love for his mother and his admiration for Charlie, his delight in the beauty of the changing seasons, his self-doubts when he becomes aware of the many forms lust and sensuality can take. Those portions of the novel dealing with John's sensitive experience of the world about him reveal just how good Bishop's prose could be when he was able to keep a tight but still unabashed rein on the impulse which moved him always toward poetry. For example, there is young John's description of the transformation wrought in his house at Christmas when his mother finally puts aside her mourning for his father's death:

> The year before, after my father's death, the house had been bare, a hushed bleakness in which my mother sat resigned, restless in black. . . . But now at Christmas, the windows were pale with frosts and gay with wreaths. The door was wreathed. And all over the house the chandeliers trailed ground pine, green claws curling as on a growing twine. The mantels were heaped in holly and on the sideboard candles rose from sombre and fragrant hemlock. Mirrored sconces wore spiny branches and reflected red wax berries. And from the ceiling in the parlor hung a huge bunch of mistletoe, sallowing slender leaves. (35-36)

Bishop's notes clearly indicate that he intended the first half of the novel to perform another function: to establish in firm outline the character of the community which finally brings Charlie Marston to trial. The Mordington of *Act of Darkness* is the product of Bishop's final fictional effort to set down a portrait of life and society in the South. Since the novel takes place in the years just before World War I, one may regard it as a further development of the sequence of stories in *Many Thousands Gone*. In the novel, Bishop intended to draw a broader and more inclusive portrait of Mordington than he had essayed previously: to dramatize the town's social structure, economic foundations, religious pretensions, moral and esthetic concerns.

He makes a valiant effort toward providing such an all-encompassing canvas. John comes into occasional contact with the mountain people who visit the town and he makes a visit to a tenant farm family. He and his friends fight with a gang from the poorer section of town; he and his grandfather visit the home of the derelict woman whose conduct scandalizes most of the citizens. John is frequently in the company of Negro servants; and his family, though not affluent, is part of the town's aristocracy. Into the story enter doctors, ministers, and lawyers; the town jailer and political boss comes from a family very like Faulkner's Snopes clan.

But all these details do not give so satisfying a picture of the society of Mordington as that found in the title story of *Many Thousands Gone*. Partly at fault is the fact that the town fades too much into the background during the long pages given over to Charlie's trial; another factor in Bishop's failure to bring the town wholly to life is the flawed narrative structure of the novel. In spite of John's sensitivity, he is not able to see and assess the total structure of the town's society; and when Bishop abandons John's point of view, he does so at the risk of violating the integrity of John's vision.

However, in spite of Bishop's failure to achieve anything on the order of Faulkner's Yoknapatawpha County or Wolfe's Altamont, he does manage to suggest something of the quality of life in a Southern town. And, even though the life of the town never becomes fully integrated with the action of the novel, Bishop manages by other means to continue and to develop his examination and assessment of the South's claims to have possessed a way of life worthy of respect and emulation. He conducts this examination not so much in terms of Mordington as a whole but by sticking closely to John's views of and reactions to those people with whom he is intimately associated: the members of his family and Virginia Crannock, the woman who cries "Rape!"

Act of Darkness is also of a piece with *Many Thousands Gone* because it presents both the virtues and the limitations of the Southern tradition. The novel, however, suggests that in the twentieth century that tradition is in the process of destroying itself. Because the staunchest representatives and defenders of the tradition are aging, John finds himself out of sympathy with them. His Aunt Maria, an old woman who watches her pennies and is in the habit of visiting watering-places in the off-season, dresses so grotesquely and has such idiosyncratic ways that John thinks: "If there had been ghosts, . . . then I am sure they would have appeared in their manners something like Aunt Maria" (19).

John's grandfather, an old man wounded during the Civil War, collects relics of his family's and his state's history, but he keeps them stored in a dusty shed along with junk tossed out of the house. The grandfather boasts that for twenty years he has not tasted whiskey before nine in the evening, but more and more he sleeps during the day and awakens only at nightfall. He dreams of writing a biography of General Charles Lee but spends most of his time attempting to untangle the fiscal indebtedness of West Virginia—a scheme which he speaks of as a selfless and dedicated act, but by which he stands to profit. Near the end of the book, when he is in the depths of his depression, John thinks of his grandfather in these terms: "My grandfather, like a spider, spun from his innards the thin threads of a tradition and, confused by his own web, talked about the West Virginia debt" (345).

In spite of their defects, though, John's grandfather and his Aunt Maria are forceful, sympathetic figures. The tradition which they represent may be aging and attenuated, but even as it is dimly reflected in the imperious old woman and the toddy-sipping old man, the tradition is productive of character and forthrightness. John's grandfather and great-aunt do not necessarily represent the Virginia tradition as ineffectual and without merit; the weaknesses of the two old people suggest instead that the tradition is humanly imperfect.

John's great-aunt and grandfather also suggest, of course, that the vitality of the Southern tradition has diminished and that it exerts little force in the modern world. The generation which succeeds them—the generation of Virginia Crannock and Caroline and Charlie Marston, John's aunt and uncle—represents the utter decline and total collapse of that tradition. (John's mother may be taken as a representative figure of the persistent worth of the Southern way of life; unfortunately, however, she remains always a shadowy figure.) John's Aunt Caroline stands at the end of a long line of fragile Southern ladies. The child which she bears Charlie is stillborn, and the quality about her which most impresses John is her sweet softness: "Her hand was soft, everything about Caroline was soft, even to the breast of peacock feathers on her toque" (37). When she is in the first months of her pregnancy and will no longer sleep with her husband, even though she clings to him unceasingly, Charlie bitterly says of her: "'... by God, you'd think we're right back in the 'sixties.... She lays down all the time and she's so fragile I'm afraid she'll break if I touch her. And with her that way, I have to be a fine old Southern gentleman.'" (62).

While Caroline's clinging softness points to the sterile foolishness of the decaying ideal of Southern womanhood, Charlie Marston and Virginia Crannock represent the disintegration of the Southern code as a guide to conduct. If one agrees with Bishop that a traditional discipline provides a way of ordering behavior, of giving meaning and coherence to instinctual life, then one may say that the two principals in the "act of darkness" represent a split in the Southern ideal of ordered behavior, a polarization of wild instinctual abandon and intellectual repression of those instincts. Virginia Crannock, unmarried at thirty-seven, lives alone in the gloomy splendor of Guyon Hall, surrounded by books and venturing out to collect wildflowers and to supervise her many charities. Born when her father was sixty-three, she is the daughter of one of the floreate Southern poets, whose verses strike John as boring and "at once too highflown in their fine sentiments and too matter-of-fact" (131).

In Virginia, the Southern tradition has become even more sterile and bootless than in Caroline; Virginia, however, wishes to cut herself off from that tradition entirely. At one point she says, "'Sometimes I wish Guyon Hall would burn down.... I should like to start all over, young and strong and ready to devote myself to what I really care for'" (189-90). At the same time caught up in and rejecting her past, she attempts to pass herself off as a modern, scientifically dispassionate woman. At certain moments, however, she realizes her emptiness. John is in

the habit of visiting her; and one day, when he has complained
of the little he seems to be accomplishing in life, she tells him
that to have accomplished nothing is better than to have nothing:
"'And you have not come to living by the clock. You don't know
what it is when the time comes and you can only look at middle
age and desire sits dumb'" (191). Because of her emptiness she
dangles herself before Charlie; and, because of her seeming self-
sufficiency, Charlie hates her and attempts to reduce her pride
and flirtatious arrogance.

Charlie Marston, who is contemptuous of Southern notions of
honor and gentility, is a man of instinct unable and unwilling to
control his strong sensuality. This sensuality makes him both
terrifying and attractive to John, who feels that "His mouth was
cruel as anything living" (27). Charlie's father had tried to
make a lawyer of him, "But Charlie had found the law absurd.
He used to break up the classes laughing at the abstruse
distinctions of his professors" (59). Later, his father obtains for
him a bureaucratic post in Washington, but he remains there for
only a year: "For he could never sit still. And he sat over a desk.
'I began to think,' he said afterward, 'that flies were crawling on
my brain'" (60).

After his marriage to Caroline, who brings him a rich farm,
Charlie finds himself somewhat. Bishop, who was inclined to
agree with the Agrarians' conviction that agriculture is one of
the essential bases of an ideal society, shows how Charlie could
find fulfillment during harvest time: "He was at his happiest
then. Flushed by the sun, sweating, his energy found its outlet
as the slow pulse of the farm was quickened that one day to
excitement in the threshing" (220). But Charlie is not able to
confine his energies to the usually placid pace of farming, and
after his wife's confinement he is unable to spend much of his
time at his country estate. Frequently, when he is carousing
about the countryside, Virginia comes to stay with Caroline, and
Charlie begins his courtship of Virginia largely out of his anger
at what he considers her invading meddlesomeness.

Bishop does not directly describe the sexual encounter between
the two, but afterward, when Charlie is in jail awaiting trial, he
confesses to John that he did make love to Virginia: "'I did in a
way. Because I hated her. But then how do I know. Maybe that
is all we can ever do to other people—violate them.'" He also
confesses to John that his act was shamefully wrong, not because

he had made love to her but because he had done so when he had no desire for her: "'Do you know how to hate? But at seventeen, I remember, that was something I know I wasn't taught. And Virginia, I went with her. But I never wanted her. And that was wrong. Do you understand? Wrong!'" (248-49).

Although John is shaken by the first news of Virginia's accusations of rape, his horror reaches its climax during the trial. Virginia's apparent calm as she neutrally describes her violation by Charlie strikes him as inhuman: "That Charlie had assaulted her in the woods seemed, I must confess, not impossible. But that she should sit there calmly describing his violence, was to me incredible" (266). Virginia's demeanor on the witness stand indicates that she now has lost all hope of ever redeeming her inner emptiness, but John finds Charlie's testimony even more unsettling. In the glare and heat of the courtroom, Charlie vacillates between malicious forthrightness and the "shame of the strongly sensual man" unable to stand off from his sensuality. Eventually, however, under the prodding of cross-examination, he speaks with abandon. He insists that Virginia had been the mastering force in their sexual encounter, that it was he who had been violated.

According to Charlie, after he had laid down beside Virginia, "He was without will, but struggled inwardly. For hating the woman, or supposing he did—for his admiration was awed before her mind—he shamelessly allowed her to complete his animal rapture. Then he stood, and saw what he had done. In the secluded woods, he swore he had maintained only a passive prowess.... Having as he thought destroyed Virginia, he now went on, corrupt with anguish, to deny his own domination as a male" (302). It is Charlie's denial of his manhood, his complete abnegation of the Southern ideal of masculinity and honor, that is most disturbing to John. In his imagination, John has become a participant in the "act of darkness," but Charlie's testimony has made that act not only senseless but terrifying: "What I could not forgive was his denying his domination over what had been done in the darkness of the woods that hot day in July. For whatever had happened, in the act I was included" (399).

After John has witnessed the disintegration of Charlie, the Southern man of action, and the utter depersonalization of Virginia, the modern Southern woman, he finds his own life meaningless. Troubled by mounting doubts about his own masculinity, doubts which Charlie has magnified, he withdraws from the company of youths his own age and spends most of his time indoors. Another summer comes, but the summer landscape no longer brings delight and hope to his maturing body: "I had no joy of that summer. All that coming to ripeness in the sun which a year before had warmed me with content or lifted me to natural and luminous joy, now left me indifferent, or worse" (344). As John, brooding apart from the life of the town, drifts slowly into an illness which doctors cannot diagnose, he begins to be oppressed by Mordington and its citizens:

> But now, being apart from the activities of the town, I saw how purposeless they were. . . . I looked now into the faces I no longer greeted. They were dull and mean. In desperate awareness, I saw discouragement reflected from the street, saw with what slow apathy the old men crawled about. Shabby, soiled decrepitudes, they went with stiff knees, and an occasional cheerfulness dribbled a brown slather of tobacco over their poor parched chins. This was the end to which I would come. . . . On the corners of the streets were these nameless old men, saving nothing out of a long life. Their progress had been only toward old age. It could scarcely have been worth the pain. (344-46)

Were this passage lifted out of context, it could certainly be taken as a final, sweeping rejection of the South. It is, to be sure, a cold and brutally unglamorous portrait of Mordington; but it must be remembered that John comes to this conclusion out of a "desperate awareness" and while he is morbidly depressed. At the end of the novel, when John finally departs from Mordington, he knows he could "never come back. What would return would be another young man who had assumed [his] name," but he is no longer filled with hatred and revulsion for the town and its people. He is no longer depressed by his memories of the sad protagonists in the drama he has been so mercilessly caught up in: "I was conscious rather of the tug on my heart of this land I was leaving and of the soft torture of my mother's love" (367-68).

While it is certainly true that *Act of Darkness* is centrally concerned with the myth of the South and while it is also true that the novel does not paint a flattering picture of Southern society, two points should be kept in mind. First, Bishop's novel, while insisting upon the decay of the Southern tradition, also makes it clear that that tradition was not without value and that the faults of the tradition merely demonstrate that no existing traditional code is entirely perfect—that, being a product of human ingenuity, it was necessarily limited by the tragic short-comings of the human condition from which it arose. At the same time, it must be remembered that Bishop is not alone among modern Southern writers in depicting the decline of the Southern tradition—that many of Bishop's contemporaries shared his belief that the "myth" of the Southern past might be utilized as a gauge by which to measure and contrast the present, even though they could at the same time hold the "myth" itself partially accountable for the failures of the present. What Louis Rubin has said of Southern writers in general is particularly true for Bishop: "The image of the heroic past renders the distraught present doubly distasteful, just as it is the guilt and falseness of this same heroic past that has caused the present."[14]

In the second place, it is unwise to look upon the novel as merely, or even primarily, concerned with the decay of tradition in the South. Of at least equal importance are three motifs which are dominant in all of Bishop's mature work. First, there is that celebration of the powers and magnificence of artistic form that John gains an awareness of only after his close encounter with death. The other two dominant motifs of the novel stress Bishop's belief that life is humanly possible only when man has accepted the inevitability of death and that life can never be complete if man does not recognize and admit the forces inherent in his sensual desires—forces at the same time life-enhancing and potentially destructive.

Although John, when sinking into his despairing illness, believes that, of all the people in Mordington, only the Charlie in whom he has now lost faith could have given him reason for wanting to live, he eventually trusts to his own strength to escape the pull of death. One night, while staying at a spa to which he has been taken by his anxious mother, he suffers an attack of dysentery brought on by sulfurous waters. As his spasms continue, John thinks that he can suffer no more and is convinced that he is dying. His mother is with him, but he insists that she leave him and pretends that the attack has passed. Afterwards he is not sure whether he forced her to leave out of "shame of nakedness" or "some remnant of animal intelligence that understood [he] must suffer alone," but in his aloneness he finally accepts death, even longs for it as a release from his suffering: "Death was ease. It was not only my pained and stricken bowels

that cried to sleep, it was my whole being that wanted to die."
After he has accepted death, however (and it should be kept in
mind that John's longing is not one for escape from life—not
what Bishop would describe as the death wish of the ascetic),
while he is lying amid the filth of his own blood and ordure,
sleep comes to him and during his sleep dawn breaks. The words
with which John closes the chapter describing his encounter with
death must certainly speak for the deepest convictions of John
Peale Bishop: "And having accepted death, I returned to life.
Life is desire" (356).

After his return to life and desire, and after he has been
thrilled by his reading of *Othello*, John is finally able to find a
release for his reawakened sexuality. In the past he has been
frightened of sex, troubled by his impulses toward homosexuality
and inhibited by notions picked up from reading poetry. Charlie's
shameful denial of his masculine assertiveness has doubly increased his sexual timidity; one need not be a Freudian to
perceive that John's illness is in large part caused by his
sexual fears.

On the day preceding his encounter with Virginia, Charlie had
taken John to a whorehouse in Hagerstown. Alone with the
prostitute selected for him, John had been humiliated to discover
he was impotent. After he has swiftly recovered from his illness,
John one day finds himself in Hagerstown with a schoolmate.
The two boys dare each other to visit the whorehouse, and this
time John finds that he is able to complete his initiation into the
rites of the "act of darkness." Once again faced with a prostitute,
he asks "only not to think"; he now knows that he may "trust" his
body, "provided no conscience intervened to destroy its honor."
John is still timid, but the whore is a professional. When she
assists him in their coupling, he is able to relive but not be
destroyed by the harsh mating of Charlie and Virginia:

> It was when her hands were on me that I knew what was again
> being accomplished was the act in the woods, that all its gestures
> must be repeated and forever repeated, the rape of the mind by
> the body. But that rape had now gone so far, I had so far
> ravished my mind, that I acquiesced in it; I was not afraid, I
> was no longer ashamed. And in the darkness with which we were
> now surrounded I knew that I had lost more than my vir-
> ginity. (366)

John's union with the prostitute is, of course, not of the same kind as the encounter in the woods. That act, if Charlie's account be true, was not a "rape of the mind by the body"; it was a violation on both his and Virginia's part of the body by the mind. John has finally come into manhood, and has begun to achieve a definition of himself as a human being by permitting the body to assert its demands against all the protestations of mind and conscience. In Bishop's view, it was only through the disciplines of art and by accession to the demands of the flesh that man could free himself—or at least give himself the illusions of freedom—from the wheel of time and the downward pull of mortality. When John leaves the whorehouse, he momentarily experiences such an illusion, and Bishop does not scoff at his sense of freedom because it is an illusion:

> The moon rode high over the blank street. I felt, not as though I were walking on air, but as though I were air. My body was light. I was sustained as a cloud is by the wind, and I recalled the sensation of those dreams in which delighted by some trick of the mind, which alone I had discovered, I could start off on a long stride and suddenly soar above the heads of the amazed crowd, staying aloft as long as I held my will and then, softly, swiftly and with lightness descend and with a soft step touch the ground. No further defeat or disillusion was possible to me; none could overcome me, I felt within myself too great strength to oppose them. (366-67)

Throughout his prose fiction, Bishop had been concerned with death, desire, and the potency of art. For the most part, he utilized the land of his birth, and that land's traditions, as a ground upon which to highlight his major themes. In *Act of Darkness*, these three themes finally unite as they work themselves out against the background of his most ambitious effort to set down the flavor and peculiarities of Southern society. *Act of Darkness* is not, as has been noted, a wholly successful novel; it is, however, an impressive novel. Undoubtedly autobiographical in many respects, its importance lies not so much in what it might seem to reveal of Bishop's own boyhood as in what it discloses of the toughness and sensitivity of his mature mind. Although the novel has few readers today and generally goes unnoticed, it does not, in spite of its flaws, deserve the neglect into which it and Bishop's other fiction have fallen.

CHAPTER 4

Bishop's Poetry

JOHN PEALE BISHOP was seriously engaged in poetry for more than thirty years, but during the greater part of his career he was content to imitate the poetic styles of his predecessors and contemporaries; not until late in his life did he begin to achieve an identifiably personal idiom and manner. Most of the critics who have examined Bishop's work have felt that the imitative quality of his poetry is a sign of his failure to achieve genuine poetic greatness. Although Allen Tate might insist that a poem in the Yeatsian manner in a book by Bishop "is as good there as it is anywhere else," most of the critics tend to echo, though with less asperity, Gregory and Zaturenska's assertion that the greater part of Bishop's verse faltered under "the strain of adapting itself to too many of the most fashionable styles of writing poetry . . . and no single poem, no matter how polished it may have seemed upon first reading, has the distinction of an individually formed taste and imagination."[1] R. W. Stallman, for instance, who is sympathetic to Bishop as a poet and who argues that the critical question when considering a poet's borrowing is whether "the derived convention, idiom or tone, has been transformed so that what has been borrowed is now integrated anew," nevertheless implies that Bishop's poetry is defective because it lacks individuality: "his style, even when it is not a borrowed idiom, is impersonal and neutral, as neutral as the style of Robert Bridges. His poetry lacks the signature of a personal idiom, an identifying voice or tone."[2]

This seeming impersonality of much of Bishop's poetry sets his work at odds with one of the primary, if not frequently stated, demands made upon modern art: that the art work express the personality—reveal the signature—of the artist. Almost thirty years ago, Allen Tate remarked, "In our age of personal expression the poet gets credit for what is 'his own': the art is not the thing, but rather the information conveyed about a unique personality."³ At present, when poets tend to write more and more about their private neuroses and the hair on their bellies, many readers may find it difficult to sympathize with Tate's private observation to Bishop after a reviewer of *Minute Particulars* had complained of the similarities between the two poets: "I still maintain that we are anonymous, and it doesn't make any difference under what name the results appear."⁴

Not at all concerned with projecting his own ego in his poetry, Bishop was still very much concerned with the problem of the *persona* in the poem. In his "Aphorisms and Notes," he observes that "The classic poet is not himself. He assumes a mask in order to speak. Behind the mask is a naked man." In Bishop's view, the purpose of the mask is to depersonalize the voice that issues forth, to translate the human utterance into an artistic statement. Of the "I" in the poem he says: "I am not the poet. I is the mask" (*CE*, 366). Bishop's view of the *persona*, while not exactly in accord with much contemporary verse, is certainly unexceptionable and he seems never to have abandoned it; he did, however, toward the end of his career, come to feel that he had perhaps not pursued ardently enough the fashioning of a mask that would suit his own poetic features. In his comments upon Tate's 1935 essay, Bishop argued that "The point is not whether an artist imitates, but whether he succeeds in imposing himself on the imitation." Looking about him at his contemporaries, he noted that "The proper procedure at present is to mark off a limited domain and exploit it." He slyly suggested that "the property sense it at the bottom of this," and then went on: "I lack the property sense, and worse I wander all over the lot." More seriously, he added, "Probably back of this is a desire to escape from myself."⁵ Then, in language which echoes his aphoristic comments on the need for a poetic mask through which the poet can speak, he confessed: "This desire were legitimately employed in fabricating masks through which to speak. Instead, I have, partially through laziness, picked up masks already there" (*BP*).

While Bishop did appropriate a wide range of existing poetic masks, he was moved to do so partly because he was, as Tate pointed out, a man and an artist who had experienced keenly the loss of order and the failure of tradition in the modern world.

Inclined to agree wholeheartedly with Tate's statement that "form is meaning and nothing but meaning,"[6] he found himself in a world where, since the collapse of the Renaissance vision of order, poets have had to accept a limited and non-catholic set of symbols and forms, have had to construct their own mythologies and forms, or have had to rely upon their own personalities to give validity to their poetic utterances. Bishop was suspicious of the individual personality and he was unable to accept wholly, though he could look back enviously upon, the various forms of traditional order which once made art vital and coherent. When Tate wrote, "More than most living poets, Bishop has felt the lack of a central source of form,"[7] he replied: "What I should like to find is a form which would impose itself. I have never found it. I doubt if the age has" (BP).

Bishop's eclecticism might most charitably be viewed as a consequence of his ceaseless search for appropriate forms. What is more, it may be argued that Bishop's work reveals a progress toward, and an attainment of, a poetic voice that is identifiably his own and one eminently right for what he had to say. Bishop wrote good, albeit unoriginal, poems as a young man; but his later poetry, with its linguistic brilliance and assured sense of form, is consistently good and less markedly imitative. He achieved his later manner by fusing his wide knowledge of the poetry of the past with his awareness of the experiments conducted successfully by modern poets. And he arrived at something of a formal substructure for his poetry by making use of his American heritage, his scholarly and personal acquaintance with the civilizations of the Mediterranean, and his meditations upon the meaning of myth.

In the following pages chief attention is given to the thematic emphases of Bishop's poetry. Since, however, one of the most fascinating aspects of his verse is his progress toward formal clarity, the roughly chronological approach employed will make clear his maturing artistry by attending to such matters as linguistic texture, verse structure, and poetic form.

I *Juvenilia and Youthful Imitations*

Bishop published his first poem one month before the first number of *Poetry: A Magazine of Verse* appeared in October, 1912. The magazine founded by Miss Monroe is frequently looked upon as the most significant herald of the poetic renaissance in America, but Bishop's "To a Woodland Pool," a pallid and limp thrice-removed imitation of Keats, would not have been at all out of place in the early numbers of *Poetry*. Bishop's sonnet opens:

> Clear placid pool, inclosed by forests dank,
> Like one fair pearl enclasped by emeralds green,
> How sweet it is upon thy mossy bank
> To lie and gaze upon thy deep serene.

The first number of *Poetry* contains a lengthy poem by Grace Hazard Conkling which is equally as strained in its inversions and archaisms as Bishop's effort. Miss Conkling addresses a pool in this fashion: "O strange ecstatic Pool, / What unknown country art thou dreaming of, / Or temple than this garden lovelier."[8]

It is not at all surprising that Bishop's youthful poem and Miss Conkling's verse, appearing in a "little magazine" which had announced as its aim the publication of "some of the best work now being done in English verse,"[9] are so much alike. The first numbers of *Poetry* no more signaled a widespread departure from moribund romanticism than the Armory Show of 1913 revealed that American painters and sculptors had wholeheartedly abandoned the picturesqueness and neoclassical sterility which characterized American art at the end of the century. Old fashions do not let go easily, and all the young men who wrought such momentous changes in American poetry had to struggle against the dead weight of the nineteenth century and against the charming artificiality of the "decadent" poets of the *fin-de-siècle*. Pound, Eliot, Ransom, Cummings, Stevens, all began in much the same fashion as Bishop did—by writing in the outmoded forms of the nineteenth century—and all had to find new forms and a new language before they could say what they had to say.

Bishop began his contributions to Princeton's student magazine, *The Nassau Literary Magazine*, very early in his freshman year. His first contributions are floreate echoes of Shelley and Poe, but it is not long before he begins to reveal, along with a continued sweetness of poetic diction, a variety of tone and an eagerness to experiment with complicated verse forms. "Tristram to Isolde," published in 1914, is a modified rondeau in which Bishop's strong sensuality begins to make itself evident in his verse; and "Rose-Dust," of 1915, recalls Swinburne both in its language and in its intricate nine-line stanzas. During his second and third years at Princeton he manifested an increasing awareness of recent modes in English and Continental poetry, but the Swinburnean influence continued to be paramount. Swinburne is almost ludicrously present in a hymn to "The Wireless Telegraph" which makes use of the stanzaic form of *Hertha;* more happily evident is his influence in the "Experiments in Classic Meters," which Tate reprints in the *Collected Poems,* and in "Faustina," a dramatic monologue in which the Roman empress wonders about her satiated loves and her lust for cruelty.

The influence of Yeats, which was to continue throughout Bishop's career, is perhaps first evident in "All Lovely Things I Love," which praises "all sweet-voiced things: / The coil of falling streams, / The honied murmurings / Of bees in their noontide dreams, / And the brush of Night's great wings," and in "The Witch's Daughter: 1692."[10] The latter poem, a modified ballad which employs a varying refrain, represents Bishop's first effort to employ "native" material in his poetry, even though the past to which he turns is that of New England and not of the South.

Bishop's knowledge of nineteenth-century French poetry, awakened under the tutelage of Christian Gauss, began to make itself felt toward the end of his third year at Princeton, when he composed four poems later included in *Green Fruit* (1917). The two poems gathered together under the title "Messalina Prepares a Festival" are still Swinburnean, but Baudelaire is also to be seen in such lines as

> The naked negress, flanked in folds of blue,
> Stands motionless, her brown skin edged with blue.
> Her breasts are pointed, heavy. Her thick lips
> Curl outward like a trumpet-flower's lips.

Baudelaire is even more evident in "Sonnet," which is a vision of a dead love with brooding eyes and tarnished cheeks who sighs, "There is no love where I have lain," and in "Mushrooms," which opens:

> Cold toadstools under moist moons growing
> Push up between rain-rusted leaves
> And rank wet growths which August eves
> Vex, when dull winds blowing
> Bring clouds of thin vibrating wings.

Bishop was also reading Gautier and Verlaine at this time ("Losses," first published in November, 1916, has as epigraph a stanza from one of the poems in *Sagesse*); perhaps the example of the French poets made him realize the foolishness of his customarily lush diction and led him to see that ordinary speech could be a proper vehicle for poetry. Not all the poems in *Green Fruit* display such an awareness, but "Boudoir"—which made its first appearance in the volume, and which may be indebted to the French poets in its use of alternating feminine and masculine rhymes—employs the speaking voice to good effect:

This was the music she loved; we heard her often,
Walking there in the green-clipt garden plots outside.
It was just at the time when the summer begins to soften,
And cicadas are shrill in the long afternoon, that she died.

The subjects of most of Bishop's apprentice verse were "literary," and all his early poems were couched in traditional, if frequently complicated, rhyme and metrical patterns. The mature Bishop always agreed with Eliot that, strictly speaking, "there is no such thing as free verse" (*CE*, 104). He came to see, of course, the possibility of achieving musicality in a poem which would have irregular line lengths and shifting meters, but the young poet was at first hesitant about embracing the metrical theories of the American advocates of free verse. The course of his conversion is to be seen in a series of poetry reviews he did for the "*Lit*" during his junior and senior years.

The first review, appearing in April, 1916, is a not very sympathetic look at Amy Lowell's *Sword Blades and Poppy Seeds*. Noting that Miss Lowell insists upon "the syntax and order of prose; upon a rejection of 'poetic' words; upon colloquial language," Bishop agrees that the "better poets have long ago left poetic license and lazy inversion to the unscrupulous poetaster." But he then argues that such poets "have also realized that the order of words and phrases in poetry should represent a more conscious arrangement than is possible in spoken language to which prose is more closely related."[11] The very next month, Bishop praised Masefield's *Good Friday and Other Poems* and concluded that, "once and for all, these sonnets should give the lie to the statement that modern thought cannot be expressed in the traditional poetic form."[12]

By the next winter, though, he had put aside much of his

suspicion of newer poetic modes. In January, 1917, he enthusi-
astically reviewed Amy Lowell's *Men, Women, and Ghosts.*
Deeming her superior to Frost and Masters, he observed that
her style, "which in the earlier volumes showed experimentation
and imitation, or at least influence of the Parnassians and
Symbolists, here appears in a complete and finished state."[13] His
last review, of John Gould Fletcher's *Goblins and Pagodas,* opens
by lamenting the current fashionable acceptance of *vers-libre*:
"Once there was a time when metre and rhyme were necessary
accompaniments to poetic expression. Now no lack of training
need hinder the fecundity of minor poets." Bishop does not see
Fletcher as such a poetaster, though, and states that "it is a joy
to find a man like John Gould Fletcher who has seized *vers libre*
as a new medium to create images of beauty, who has come to
it endowed with a high rhythmic sense, and who has bestowed
upon it the unremitting toil which has always accompanied the
making of every genuine work of art."[14]

The month after his second Lowell review the "*Lit*" printed
Bishop's "Campbell Hall," an irregularly rhymed poem with
irregular line lengths. "February 1917," first published in *Green
Fruit,* is a freely structured poem which does away with rhyme
altogether. However, of the twenty-seven poems in Bishop's first
volume, only five are in the free-verse manner. For the most part,
Bishop's experiments in the new medium are stiff and awkward;
the lines almost always conclude with full syntactic stops and
the devices he employs to marshal his verses are not at all subtle.
For example, the opening lines of "In the Beginning" employ a
heavyhanded alliteration:

> I had dreamed that Love would come under broad pennons of
> gold,
> With rumbling of ponderous drums and conches braying,
> Straying of crimson,
> Bickering of banners blown to vermilion and gold,
> With brown-burnt faces under barbaric turbans,
> And a tumult of hoofs upon stony pavements.

Even in their awkwardness, though, Bishop's early poems in the
new manner make evident his desire to impose order upon his
verse; and certain lines from the poems move with a deliberate
beauty. "In Such a Garden" closes with the sureness of "There
should be peacocks on the open grass / And a great basin to

blur / Its shadows of dark green and pallors of silver." And the final lines of "In the Beginning" almost redeem its opening: ". . . quietly as a girl who walks / With bare feet over the warm grass / In a night of moths and roses."

The poems in *Green Fruit* are as consciously "literary" in subject matter as they are in verse structure. Princeton is the backdrop for some of the poems, but the college and town are generally seen through a nineteenth-century haze. If one excludes the four "Princeton" poems from the accounting, there are only seven other poems which one might classify as having emerged from Bishop's non-bookish background and experience—and all these are strongly colored by the books he had come in contact with.

French accents hover over "Boudoir," and there is a strong echo of Webster in the last line of the poem: "Give me your hand. She was lovely. Mine eyes blind." "The Triumph of Doubt" finds within the American landscape images for the speaker's wearied disillusionment, but Masefield and Thompson seem to be the guiding spirits of the poem. Even the non-Princeton pieces in the "Poems out of Jersey and Virginia" section are self-consciously literary. The fungi in "Mushrooms" are more decadent than Virginian, and there is much more Keats than sharecropper in "Endymion in a Shack." There seems to be a touch of the sharecropper in "Sights: Eastern Virginia," an imitation ballad in dialect; but the language is very awkwardly handled, and Bishop rarely afterward attempted to employ in verse an extreme form of vernacular idiom. The poem is more indebted to the nineteenth-century English and Scottish ballad makers than it is to Bishop's knowledge of American speech patterns. Such literary influences are even more apparent in the other ballad, "Leaf-Green," a fairy legend which comes straight from Yeats and Stevenson.

Of all the poems dealing with the world Bishop knew, only "Boudoir" and "Miss Ellen" approach success. The latter poem, the most satisfactory in *Green Fruit,* has much in common with the "Portraits" of genteel New England society turned out by the youthful T. S. Eliot.[15] Miss Ellen, a spinster who presents an active and gossipy front to the world, betrays the terror behind her façade by incessant knitting and by lapses into dreams of youth when she is alone with the keepsakes of her maidenhood. The language of the poem is low-keyed, the four-stress lines move easily across rhymes, and the mocking tone of the poem is well conveyed by the easy grotesquerie of certain of the rhymes:

> Then tea comes in with squares of toast,
> Dusted with sweetened cinnamon,
> And cakes which are Miss Ellen's boast
> Whenever cakes are touched upon.

Although perhaps a bit pat in its two-part structure, the poem is nevertheless masterful in its assemblage of snippets of polite speech and is a significant anticipation of Bishop's mature concern with the decayed elegance of Southern culture.

Green Fruit is of interest mainly as a document which reveals Bishop's poetic gropings and as a record of some of the influences impinging upon the new American poetry. The poems were written over a span of only two or three years, but their maker had traversed several decades of poetry in putting them together. He had begun as imitator of an outworn sensibility and had ended by being caught up in the ferment of contemporary verse. Bishop was still enamored of a vision of beauty he had caught from books which moved and excited him, but in 1917 he knew that he could no longer dally in the world of Swinburne and Gautier. His sense of loss, but also his knowledge of the inevitability of that loss, are explicit in the last poem in *Green Fruit,* an epistle to his friend Townsend Martin. The poem notes that, once, he had dreamed of exotic gifts for his friend: "ambergris and cinnamon, / Couched in ebon coffers or in ivory divine." Now, however, the only gifts he can proffer are "Spotted fruit and bitter fox-grapes, plundered by the rain." The poem is almost saccharinely juvenile in its forlorn farewell to "spring-delighted gardens"; in the years to come, while he still dreamed of "ambergris and cinnamon," Bishop would learn to make wiser and better poems of spoiled fruit and rain-plundered gardens.

In the last line of the last poem in *Green Fruit*, after his abandonment of "cinnabar and cassia," Bishop remarks, "I go another way." The way was toward war and an even wider knowledge of modern verse, but the poems he published in the next half-dozen years were as tentative in their imitations of other poets as was his college verse. The poems reflect his brush with death and his youthful disillusionment, but the impress of

Yeats, Pound, Eliot, and Laforgue (and a diverse host of other poets) is so unmodified that hardly any achieves a life of its own. The uncollected poems of this period are both fragmentary and preciously artificial, and only one of the more ambitious poems in *The Undertaker's Garland* (1922) manages to escape from diffuseness and prolixity.

The extent of Bishop's borrowings is readily apparent in the two "Sonnets from Porphyrio the Mad Prince to the Princesse Lointaine." Pound, Eliot, and Laforgue seem equally responsible for the ironic tone, the "hard" vocabulary, and the wide-ranging allusions:

> Your hair is rufulous as the puffed rust
> Blebbing a musket stock, vermicular
> As the crimped locks stringing from the coif are
> In Niccoló Fiorentino's bust
> Of D'Este.

His indebtedness to the post-Prufrockian Eliot is even more pronounced in "To Helen"—to be noted in the epigraph from Tourneur, in the use of laconic quatrains, in a direct echo from "The Hippopotamus," and in the structure of the poem, which moves abruptly through a series of seemingly dissociated images. "Song" is a quite different sort of poem, but behind it lurk the diction and attitude of Yeats's post-impressionist verse:

> Who is there to defame her
> Although she is faithless?
> I have heard no man name her
> But at once he was breathless
> To say that the beauty she has
> Is more terrible than white brass.

Nevertheless, imitative though these poems are, there is an increasing skill in the use of rhyme and in the maintenance of movement through the lines. There is a loose freedom about the verse that had been lacking in Bishop's earlier poetry, a freedom which was perhaps engendered by Bishop's acknowledgement of his own sensuality—a sensuality now less encumbered by pastiches of Swinburne and Baudelaire. This sensuality is figured well in "Always from My First Boyhood" and in "A Small Oration to the Sun." And one gets a foretaste of Bishop's later erotic poetry in a short poem in *Vanity Fair* which escaped inclusion in the *Collected Poems*:

> I look at you
> And tremble.
> I am become as a naked swimmer
> In the summer dawn.[16]

Apart from their subject matter, most of Bishop's poems in *The Undertaker's Garland* have little interest—and at this late date it is difficult to become exercised about Satanism, vignettes of death, and the efforts of the young Wilson and Bishop to *épater* the American middle class. Most of the poems are tediously long (with a diction that seems a throwback to Masefield and Thompson) and without any firm sense of structure. The only exception is "The Death of a Dandy," which also happens to be the only poem that achieved separate publication.

Like many of Bishop's other poems written during this period, "The Death of a Dandy" shows definite traces of Eliot. The situation of the poem (an old man reliving his past) recalls "Gerontion"; moreover, Eliot's poem is probably responsible for the irregular line lengths and stanzaic groupings Bishop employs. There are certainly verbal echoes of "Gerontion" in the poem:

> What thoughts should an old man have
> In the London autumn
> Between dusk and darkness?
> Behind the shrunken eyelids, what apparitions?
> What pebbles rattle in a dry stream?

And the opening lines seem to have been shaped by the stage setting of section two of *The Waste Land*:

> The exquisite banality of rose and ivory:
> Shadows of ivory carved into panels, stained
> And decayed in the moulding; rose-colour looped
> Casting a shadow of mauve; blown cherubs
> Bulging in silver,
> Lift six tapers to the lighted mirror.

In spite of the debt to Eliot, however, one may say that the poem achieves a success of its own: it manages to weld language, structure, and form into a coherent whole. There is a subtle modulation and grouping of the irregular lines, and the poem demonstrates Bishop's increasingly skillful command of verbal music. Babette Deutsch has pointed out that the mature Bishop was a deft manipulator of fricative consonants,[17] and the following passage shows that by 1922 he had learned how to incorporate delightful sound within the movement of smoothly flowing verse:

> The chamfered fall of silken rose—
> Muffling London and the autumn rain—
> Lifts and recurves,
> A beautiful young man,
> Naked, but for a superb white tiewig,
> Moves in with slow pacings of a cardinal
> Dreaming on his cane.

"The Death of a Dandy" is also Bishop's own in subject matter and in his attitude toward it. It genuinely reveals his admiration for certain periods of the past and his respect for hardly won and finely maintained codes of etiquette—while at the same time it recognizes that all upholders of tradition can only momentarily stay their own progress toward dissolution, that, beneath his elegant costume, even the dandy must shrivel into decay. "The Death of a Dandy" is a rendering in poetry of a set of attitudes he had expressed some time before in a *Vanity Fair* essay. He saw dandyism as a "meaningless protest against a life without meaning," but he prized the futility of the dandy's protests above the progressivism of the inventors and industrialists of the nineteenth century. Of the creed of progress, he said: "I shall not subscribe"; instead, he chose to honor the dandies who "regarded living as an art; possibly, since life seemed to them useless, as a fine art."[18] Bishop's poem registers the futility of its protagonist's fine gestures, but it also sympathizes with the dandy's efforts to "escape this disappointing body / Punily erect, patched with scant hair."

In the future, Bishop would deal frequently with the twin themes of human frailty and man's struggles to offset and transcend his bondage to time; "The Death of a Dandy" may therefore be seen as anticipatory of the matter of much of Bishop's mature verse. In like fashion, the careful craftsmanship of the poem heralds the technical mastery which Bishop was to display during the next two decades.

II Now With His Love

Although he continued to work at his poetry throughout the
1920's, Bishop did not publish another volume of verse until the
1930's when, in quick succession, he brought out *Now With His
Love* (1933) and *Minute Particulars* (1935). Several of the
poems in the second volume were written in the 1920's, but there
is nevertheless a marked difference between the structural and
thematic emphases of the two books. *Now With His Love*
continues to show the stresses engendered by Bishop's quest for
appropriate form; many of the poems reveal unassimilated borrowings from other poets, and there is an almost equal division
between poems employing irregular verse structures and those
making use of regularly patterned stanzas and meters. Many of
the most successful poems emerge from the dominant theme in
the volume: the values of sensuality in a world of seeming
chaos. And many of the best poems achieve their effects by
imitation of, or reference to, the effects of the plastic arts. Such
concerns are apparent in *Minute Particulars,* but the volume is
marked more by an attention to American culture and by
Bishop's growing fascination with the function and meaning of
myth. Equally as important, the second volume is less imitative,
and most of the poems employ regular verse structures.

The opening poem of *Now With His Love,* "Speaking of
Poetry," shows how well he could handle irregular meters. His
command of phrasing and musical progression is clearly evident
in this passage:

> Desdemona was small and fair,
> delicate as a grasshopper
> at the tag-end of summer: a Venetian
> to her noble fingertips.

For Bishop's purposes, such a structure is particularly appropriate; with it he declares his independence of the Shakespearean
drama which provides the major symbols of his poem. One might
also say that the structure, in its mediation between freedom
and regularity, is an appropriate reflection of the tension in the
poem between two of its dominant symbols: the barbarous
Othello and the delicate Desdemona.

Once the excellence and rightness of the verse are admitted, one's attention legitimately shifts to a consideration of what the verse says. And the poem is important because it presents symbolically one of Bishop's primary convictions about art—and, by extension, life. The burden of the poem is given in the opening lines: "The ceremony must be found / that will wed Desdemona to the huge Moor." Desdemona is feminine, the product of centuries of culture, and a careful artisan (she has three times imitated in needlework her father's shield and three times pulled out her stitches "to begin again, each time / with diminished colors"); but as a symbolic figure within the poem she is not sufficient to herself. She must be mated to the savagery of Othello, who values an embroidery not so much "for the subtlety of the stitches, / but for the magic in it." The fruit of their union, or perhaps the very nature of it, will presumably be akin to the most valid forms of poetry: it will be both feminine and masculine, cultured and savage, conscious and dionysiac, esthetic and magical. It is important, however, to keep in mind that in Bishop's scheme it is Desdemona, the craftsman, who is in the foreground, and the poem does not so much invoke a taming of Othello as a necessary violation of Desdemona. For Bishop, poetry does not begin in savagery; but it must mate with savagery if it is to be anything more than mere needlework.

Just as the poem focuses upon Desdemona, the product of Venetian culture, so also does it insist upon the need for a "ceremony" to effect the union between culture and savagery. It is not enough that the lovers "meet, naked, at dead of night / in a small inn on a dark canal." The consequence of such an unceremonious coupling will be, again, the death of Desdemona. The union must take place, and it must be sexual; but in order for it to be lasting and fruitful the union must be celebrated publicly and solemnly. And there must be at least four components of the ceremony: it must be

> Traditional, with all its symbols
> ancient as the metaphors in dreams;
> strange, with never before heard music; continuous
> until the torches deaden at the bedroom door.

The ceremony which will wed the opposite natures of Desdemona and Othello is itself composed of contrarieties, and its seemingly divergent elements reflect the paradoxes involved in

Bishop's attitudes toward life and art. It must be "traditional," a product of human experience, and its symbols must be "ancient." At the same time, it must be "strange," and its symbols must express the truth of dreams. It must be embodied in music and it must have continuity, but it must also hint at "never before heard music" and must cease when the lovers pass from public ceremony to private mystery. While the potency which the ceremony ensures can only come as a result of the ritual, it is not identical with the enactment of the ritual. And the poetry and renewal of life of which the poem speaks are not to be found singly in either the delicacy of Desdemona or the animality of Othello, but in the fusion of the two. It is characteristic of Bishop that he focuses upon Desdemona and that he insists upon ceremony and order, but it is also characteristic that he demands her marriage to brute strength and magic—and that the ceremony which he imagines is as strange and mysterious as it is traditional.

For the attentive reader of modern poetry, it takes no great effort to make out the drift of meaning in "Speaking of Poetry"—to see that it is, first of all, a statement about the elements which fuse to form a valid work of art. One could, however, read the poem as a statement about culture in general—see Desdemona as the carrier of civilized values who must be wedded to barbarism if the civilization of which she is the symbol is not to lapse into mannerism and sterility. One must also admit that no statement *about* the poem is going to exhaust its meaning or even fully characterize it. What is involved here, however, is not merely the fact that one cannot paraphrase a poem; the difficulty is that one cannot be fully sure of the meaning of the poem. And the difficulty rises out of the formal strategy of the poem. In its form, the poem is an analogy expressed in symbolic language. The symbols of the poem, however, are not fixed, and the analogy is hinted at merely in the poem's title. The poem itself does not draw any conclusions from the analogy; the reader must elucidate the symbols and he alone must make the connections between the symbolic concreteness of the poem and the abstractions with which he presumes it ultimately concerns itself.

The strategy of most poetry prior to the twentieth century was quite different. In addition to having a fund of symbolism whose meaning was more accessible, earlier poets generally made use of a strategy one might characterize as "rhetorical": they set up a situation within their poetry and then followed the logic of that situation to a stated conclusion. Generally, the *persona* indicated to the reader what his attitude toward the situation ought to be, and the meaning of the poem was generally made clear by the utterances of the poem. Modern poetry, however, is apt to proceed by indirection. And even when the modern poet is alarmingly direct—as in the case of the lyric of personal expression—he is not inclined to comment on the emotions and situations presented; in its nakedness, the direct statement is likely to be as troubling as symbolic indirection.

In their double quest for indirection and startling directness, modern poets have turned to several modes of utterance: the straightforward lyric statement; the concrete presentation of an object, situation, or event—in which the concern of the poet is focused as much upon the method of presentation as the object or situation being described; the seemingly direct statement (of either lyric impulse or dramatic incident) twisted and given a new direction by ironies hinted at by the language and imagery of the poem; the dramatic monologue; the poem which is essentially a symbolic statement having as its end an analogy between the formal statement and an abstract condition outside the poem; and, finally, the longer poem of several parts, in which it is likely that various modes will be mingled and in which it is unlikely that there will be an evident tissue of connective logic between the several parts.

Bishop was never totally averse to the principle of rhetorical organization, and the meaning of much of his mature poetry may be grasped quite readily. But in *Now With His Love* he essays all but the last of the several modes enumerated above. The largest single category is composed of lyrics of direct statement which have as their subjects the complex of themes hinted at by the quotation from "The Knight's Tale" which serves as the general epigraph for the volume: "What is this world? What asketh man to have? / Now with his love, now in the colde grave, / Allone, withouten any compaignye."

These poems betray a fascination with death and with sensual love; frequently they are hymns to love which spring out of the awareness of death. This is particularly true of "And When the Net Was Unwound Venus Was Found Ravelled With Mars," an account of a wartime assignation. The speaker of the poem, the male lover who is almost undone by the tawdry inn and the piglike old woman who shows the lovers to their room, yet manages to keep his thinking concentrated "on one point / that burned upon [his] thighs, until it seemed / the very center whence they wheel, all fiery / and all turning stars." When the lovers undress, the woman's nakedness reveals her as a being totally separate from the cheap furnishings of the room, a woman formed by the antique graces of Mediterranean culture:

> It seemed her body had been burned
> by blue Italian ponds
> and moving kept such equipose as though
> she had learned of old bronze
> bright breast and the thigh like a boy's.

When they make love, it is with "perfect lust," and their union is like the return of Proserpine to Aetna. After the account of their lovemaking, the speaker notes that all this happened "in the time of the long war" when the old men came always to the same decision: "More of the young / must die." The poem concludes, however, by asserting the triumph of the young lovers over the designs of the old men: "Of them I remember and their nights / her warmth as of a million suns."

The two other poems which seem to have been inspired by Bishop's wartime experiences are more elegiac in tone. One, "In the Dordogne," describes a billet in an old chateau and speaks of the dead buried "close to the old wall / within a stone's throw of Perigord / under the tower of the troubadours." This poem achieves its effects quietly, and the monstrousness of the deaths suffered by the young men rotting in their graves is made clear by the beauty of the imagery describing the landscape in which they lie buried:

> in a land of small clear silent streams
> where the coming on of evening is
> the letting down of blue and azure veils
> over the clear and silent streams
> delicately bordered by poplars.

The other, "Young Men Dead"—which is undoubtedly indebted to Yeats for its half rhymes, short lines employing two and three stresses, and the vertical movement down those lines—is nevertheless a very good poem in its own right. The three young men who figure as symbols of all those dead in the war are fully and separately realized in a few short lines, and the diction manages to be stately and dignified even while it daringly employs simultaneously such a recondite word as "contumelious" and expressions bordering on slang. The skillful use of an initial "And" to introduce the sections characterizing the last two dead soldiers and the final comment of the speaker unites all four soldiers; this seemingly simple technical maneuver makes all the more poignant the statement which concludes the poem: "And I who have most reason / Remember them only when the sun / Is at his dullest season."

When Bishop prepared his *Selected Poems* in 1941, he wisely excluded the two other poems in *Now With His Love* which might be catalogued as lyrics proceeding from an awareness of death: "Wish in the Daytime" and "Night." He saw fit, however, to remove only one of the several love lyrics in the 1933 volume. The poem set aside was "To His Late Mistress," which is flawed by the unsuccessful grafting of references from *Hamlet* onto what is essentially an imitation of the amatory lyrics of the troubadour poets. He properly retained, however, another poem which owes much to the tradition of courtly love. "Fiametta," written in the early 1920's, is one of Bishop's finest poems. Its success depends partly upon the richness of the language used to characterize the young maiden praised by the poem and partly upon the subtle variations in the rhyme and metrical scheme of the three stanzas. The couplet rhymes that conclude the first two stanzas are slightly off ("duller" and "color"; "lady" and "body"), but the discordances are resolved by the strictness of the final rhyme—between "praised" and "upraised." There are close syntactic and metrical parallels between the first two six-line stanzas, but after its first two lines the third stanza varies considerably. The third line is extended, and the last two lines invert the established pattern of a four-stress line followed by one of three stresses. "Fiametta" shows how Bishop had learned to modify metrical structures to avoid monotony and make the variations within the verse a significant part of the poem's meaning.

Almost as fine as "Fiametta" are three poems which must have been prompted by Bishop's love for his wife. "Epithalamium" is a two-quatrain poem which manages to capture both the delights and the terrors of sexual love. The second quatrain intensely underlines man's awareness of the narrow borderline between life and death when caught up in the frenzy of sexual passion:

> My breath abandoned me and my breath failed
> And silence came all sighing to my mouth.
> My knees went down before her naked feet.
> Love was the cry recovered me from death.

What is most arresting in the "Metamorphoses of M" are Bishop's command of a swiftly moving blank-verse line and the conceits that underlie the two poems. There are three sentences and thirteen lines in the first poem; two sentences and eleven lines in the second. In the first poem the sentences increase in length as the tension of the poem mounts; in the second, the first sentence takes up only half a line while the rest of the poem develops the opening statement in one long onrushing sentence.

In the first poem of "Metamorphoses...," Bishop employs the conceit of envisioning his love's naked feet as shod by "Venetian artisans" who had been all night awake, "painting in gold, / To set your beauty on appropriate heels." The other poem, which echoes Antony's praise of Cleopatra in its opening sentence, "Your beauty is not used," goes on to describe the loved one as rising each morning "splendidly renewed" before turning to the world of medieval legend for the conceit with which to drive home the lyric assertion of the loved one's unchanging beauty:

> ... even the unicorn that savage beast
> If he should startle on you fresh from light
> Would be so marvelled by virginity
> That he would come, trotting and mild,
> To lay his head upon your fragrant lap
> And be surprised.

When Bishop put together his *Selected Poems,* he included from *Now With His Love* only one of the four poems which might be classified as efforts to achieve neutral descriptions of objects or events. The three left out—"This Is the Man," "Account of a Crime," and "My Grandfather Kept Peacocks"—are interesting today only because they reflect certain themes which engaged their author. "This Is the Man" describes an ugly European who reveals an instinct for beauty; "Account of a Crime" narrates an episode of violence rising out of the tedium of modern life; and "My Grandfather Kept Peacocks" testifies to Bishop's involvement with his ancestry and the decaying traditions of the South.

The salvaged poem, "Still-Life: Carrots," is presumably an effort at iconic verse—that is, poetry which attempts to approximate in words the content and manner of the plastic arts.[19] Bishop's poem is, however, unlike most iconic verse in that he evokes the still-life solely in terms of metaphor. Just as the painter has transformed the carrots by fixing them on canvas, so Bishop suggests their new quality of being by comparing them to "Tritons / Just rising from the uneven wave." In his effort to convey the vigor of the composition, he turns almost instinctively to the Mediterranean world of myth; and in this very short poem he is able to fuse, and convey to the reader, his high respect for the powers of art, the warmth of his affection for the Mediterranean, and his sense of the permanent meaning of myth.

In *Now With His Love* there are several poems in the ironic mode, but Bishop was never fully at ease when he assumed this stance. When he did so, he was too prone to ape the mannerisms of other poets, and not one of the five "ironic" poems of the 1933 volume deserves much praise. Curiously enough, all five have their locales in Europe, and three are about English and American sojourners abroad.

"October Tragedy," the longest poem in the volume, is a narrative dealing with the discovery of a girl's corpse and the consequent unraveling of the causes of her death. Although interesting as an indication of Bishop's double concern with love and death, it is flaccid in its technique and almost sentimentally heavy-handed in its ironies. "Martyr's Hill," an account of a young man's shaky progress through a Parisian dawn, is flawed by its extreme dependence upon Laforgue and, possibly, Apollinaire: "The little whores have all gone in / And gray as mice / Creep to some hole stuffed against today." The other three poems, which describe the antics of English and American tourists in Europe, are indebted to Bishop's American contemporaries. "An English Lady" and "Château à Vendre" owe too much to Pound and Eliot; for "Riviera," Bishop borrows from Cummings disordered syntax and typographical idiosyncrasies.

The two dramatic monologues in *Now With His Love* do not measure up to Bishop's later efforts in the mode, but "Easter Morning" is of interest as an index of how continuing was the influence of Eliot upon Bishop, and the "Portrait of Mrs. C" has value as one of Bishop's earliest efforts to come to grips with the decaying traditions of the South. The old lady who rambles to herself in the poem is a counterpart of the doughty old Mrs. Doyne in his short story, "The Corpse in the House." She knows that her own generation after the Civil War was "absurd" in its "futility" and "too fine / In the discrimination of despair," but the poem makes it clear that Bishop's sympathy is with the old woman, who insists:

> For God in Heaven!
> What is there to this life unless we can
> Endow it with some rarity beyond
> The common run?

Apart from the poems of lyric sentiment, the most successful pieces in *Now With His Love* are those which are essentially symbolic statements. There are, however, several poems which do not fit into the categories marked out, and these should be discussed briefly. First of all, there are three epigrammatic poems which show Bishop's skill at compression and his ability to turn a pithy phrase. And there are two rather unclassifiable poems which are significant mainly as indicators of Bishop's thematic concerns and of some of the dominant influences upon his art. "Down!" is a semidramatic monologue which borrows its images from Canto XIII of the *Inferno* and has as its theme sexual jealousy; "Twelfth Night," obviously influenced by both Yeats and Eliot, is flawed by the anomalous and unrealized position of the *persona* who describes and comments upon the action. Finally, there are several poems which are primarily rhetorical and discursive in structure, which set up a situation and then comment upon it openly.

The most elusive among these is "The Ancestors," a piece whose opening lines are reminiscent of Allen Tate's similarly titled poem.[20] The first two stanzas describe a feeling of oppression which invests an old house on a stormy night; the concluding two stanzas ask "Why should the wind rise now?" and then move outward to speculate on the plight of the unhoused poor and upon the "calm" which the mind experiences when it contemplates "the stone ease / Of passions rising in the sculptured tomb!" Similar rhetorical structures shape "Aliens," a not very good attempt to delineate the plight of dwellers in modern cities, and also "Hunger and Thirst," a more satisfying poem about the perverse and cannibalistic instincts of both men and animals. It proceeds by cataloguing various instances of unholy appetite and then concludes: "We too have known within our cell / Voices entreat us that we feed / On flesh whose bone we loved too well."

A highly rhetorical pattern is also evident in the most moving poem in the volume: "Beyond Connecticut, Beyond the Sea." This rumination upon Bishop's ancestry and posterity is dignified but at the same time precise in its command of the idiom of speech:

> When I look into my sons' eyes I see
> The color of seawater, blue
> Under cold shores. Their bodies will be tall.
> Their hair has come to them from far off,
> Washing like seaweed through diverse waters.

The meaning of the poem is open and obvious, but its quality is not simple. It is, by turns, reflective, humorous, aspirant, and heroic. It shows an awareness of death but also asserts the continuity of life. A private poem which manages to make a public statement, it fully demonstrates—as do several of Bishop's later poems—that a modern poet may risk a direct statement without falling into banality and windy rhetoric.

The modern poem which is essentially a symbolic statement (that is, one which is not reducible to the statements within the poem) frequently proceeds by linking within a single form seeming incongruities of statement and imagery and depends for its meaning on the interaction between, and progressive development of, the various elements of the poem. Bishop only infrequently employs this strategy, preferring (as in the case of "Speaking of Poetry") to construct a single coherent image, but *Now With His Love* contains a perfect example of the type: "The Truth About the Dew."

This poem, which appeared first in the May, 1932, issue of *Poetry* devoted to Southern verse, is partly an outgrowth of Bishop's enthusiastic reading of the Agrarians' manifesto, *I'll Take My Stand;* and the reader undoubtedly needs to be aware of the particular context of the poem before he can be very sure of its meaning.[21] The first three stanzas present three contrasting images of the dew, as seen by three different representative figures of the South. Maria, who represents the romanticizing impulses of the white Southern aristocracy, "sees the dew as green." Opposed to Maria is the Negress Calinda; for her "dew is black." Another angle of vision is provided by the small farmer, Abner, who "could have sworn / Dew on the long corn leaves was white." The final image of the poem, presumably the one which supersedes the three that have gone before, is provided by a "small / Lascivious rabbit" who shivers a cobweb and lets fall "Myriads of rainbows from the dew."

The statement which the poem makes is that the view of the human inhabitants of the South is necessarily limited; the rabbit, however,—particularly since he has definite affinities with the *lièvre* in Rimbaud's "Après le Déluge" and with Stevens' "A Rabbit as King of the Ghosts"—may be taken as a symbol of the encompassing poetic imagination, not tied down to any particular set of biases and able to bathe the world in the myriad colors of the rainbow.

Bishop's more usual habit is to develop a single symbolic situation embodied in images more obviously interconnected than those found in "The Truth About the Dew." He does not always manage to create memorable poetry when he proceeds in this manner ("Admonition" and "Encounter" are not very good poems), but he succeeds more often than not. "Behavior of the Sun" makes use of the world of boyhood to comment upon the differences between scientific investigation and poetic imagination, and "This Dim and Ptolemaic Man" beautifully employs the image of a middle-aged farmer crouched upon a "rattly Ford" to suggest the madness of modern man's awed confidence in science and technology. And this technique of symbolic elaboration provides the formal substance of one of Bishop's best and most frequently anthologized poems, "The Return."

"The Return" employs a form like that of "Speaking of Poetry." Ostensibly an utterance about the despair which afflicts the citizens of a Roman town when they become aware of the imminent collapse of their civilization, it is in effect a commentary upon modern civilization. The form of the poem is, as Bishop remarked privately to Tate, "an elaborate simile with one member of the comparison kept in silence." Bishop did not want his poem taken as an insistence that "modern civilization must collapse," but he did hold that "when a civilization collapses these are the phenomena to be observed" (*BP*).

Tate remarks that "As a feat of historical insight the 'form' of 'The Return' is commonplace; yet the poem is distinguished."[22] It is distinctive for several reasons, but three stand out. First, the speaking voice of the poem addresses itself consistently to a description of the collapsing world of Rome while it also suggests the analogy with modern cultural disintegration. Second, the unrhymed, basically iambic pentameter quatrains are remarkable for their metrical variety and for their command of an enjambment that carries steadily forward the pulse of hysteria in the poem:

> Night and we heard heavy and cadenced hoofbeats
> Of troops departing: the last cohorts left
> By the North Gate. That night some listened late
> Leaning their eyelids toward Septentrion.

Finally, and most importantly, the language of the poem is so densely connotative that its symbols become almost tactilely objective; in Tate's words, "The poet has manipulated language into painting."[23] Bishop's virtuoso handling of language—coupled with his predilection for embodying the materials of his poem in a sensuous medium that suggests the effects of the plastic arts (in *Now With His Love,* the poem bore this epigraph: "After a phrase by Giorgio di Chirico")—gives "The Return" a *presence* that defies paraphrase and makes the poem reverberate with a vitality that transcends meaning. This quality, to be found throughout the poem, is most evident in the last stanza, which describes how man's efforts to construct a culture of forms and traditions are finally frustrated by the relentless forces of nature:

> Temples of Neptune invaded by the sea
> And dolphins streaked like streams sportive
> As sunlight rode and over the rushing floors
> The sea unfurled and what was blue raced silver.

The three other symbolic poems in *Now With His Love*— "Ode," "Ballet," and "Perspectives are Precipices"—are even more intimately linked with certain examples of modern painting than is "The Return." Although they are not necessarily imitations of particular paintings, they are good examples of iconic verse that suggests the subject matter and manner characteristic of the work of a particular painter or group of painters.

The "Ode" is perhaps most important as one of Bishop's earliest efforts to bring into focus his awareness of the tensions between Christianity and Mediterranean mythology, but it also reflects his admiration for the great canvases of Picasso's "Roman" period. The three feminine deities who haunt the speaker's imagination, and who presumably are counterparts of the Greek Moerae and Roman Parcae, are imaged not as Hesiod presented them but in guises similar to those adopted by the giant women who loom so ominously in such Picasso paintings as the "Three Bathers" of 1920 and the "Seated Bather" of 1929. The first section describes all three goddesses as having "grave knees" and as watching with "perpetual stare" through "parrot eyes." The following three sections present individual images of the three sister goddesses. One of them "sits divine in weeping stone / On a small chair of skeleton / And is most inescapable." The second "has a face burned hard / As the red Cretan clay"; wearing a "white torso scarred / With figures like a calendar," she "sits among broken shafts / Of stone." The third is presented by means of a brief but arresting visual image: "The last has idiot teeth / And a brow not made / For any thoughts, but suffering."

Since Bishop knows full well that he is writing a poem and not drawing a picture, he takes advantage of the temporal shifts and multiple points of view possible with words (the bulk of the section devoted to the third sister is given over to the chant she mutters in "idiot singing"); but the primary impact of the poem results from his vivid rendering of the weighty presence of the three goddesses. And it is his successful presentation of the three as "Phantasmal marbles" that makes possible the violent shift of tone in the last section, when the speaker refers to "One who might have saved / Me from the grave dissolute stone / And parrot eyes." The starkness of the conclusion is both reinforced and made supportable by the imagery of bones and ruins carried over from the preceding sections: "Christ is dead. And in a grave / Dark as a sightless skull He lies / And of his bones are charnels made."

"Ballet" and "Perspectives Are Precipices" are verbal renderings of the world of surrealistic paintings. "Ballet," the less finished of the two, assembles reminders of the work of di Chirico, Dali, and Picasso—and is also reminiscent of the stage settings and choreography of Diaghilev's Ballet Russe. Its force is blunted, however, by an excessive attention to the mere rendering of details and by an almost fuzzy dislocation of syntax and structure. The disorganized structure, designed to convey the poem's dreamlike content, calls too much attention to itself and does little to translate whatever meaning might be implicit in the nightmarish action. It is likely that the ultimate meaning is to be derived from the contrast between the concluding image of the sea and the foregoing images of social and esthetic disorder, but it is also possible that the poem is an experiment in pure iconic verse: that it is merely an approximation of the *mise en scène* of surrealistic painting.

Bishop's correspondence with Tate makes clear the debt of "Perspectives Are Precipices" to the art of Salvador Dali (*BP*), but the poem is not merely a rendering of Dali's hallucinatory landscapes. Its success depends largely upon the italicized echoes from the folk tale of Bluebeard, and it is also important to keep in mind the double fact that Bishop's visual images are verbally rendered and that he takes full advantage of the strictly literary devices of meter and rhyme. The refrain from the legend of Bluebeard has a double function: it serves to heighten the terror emanating from the reader's awareness of the oppressive landscape, and it also enables him to bring into human focus the perspective which structurally orders the poem. The particularly literary quality of the imagery is to be perceived not only in the precisely employed latinity of much of the diction but also in such metaphors as "a distance of black yews / Long as the history of the Jews" and in such complex images as "I see a road sunned with white sand, / Wide plains surrounding silence." Once the essentially literary nature of the poem has been stressed, however, it must not be denied that "Perspectives Are Precipices" depicts a symbolic landscape very similar to those encountered in Dali's canvases, landscapes which depict, in startling clarity, figures fixed and held in the grasp of overpowering space.

Bishop's essay, "Poetry and Painting," stresses his belief that poets, as well as painters, may avail themselves of spatial images; but he also notes that in painting such images occur simultaneously while poetry can present them only in succession (*CE*, 182). "Perspectives Are Precipices" presents a succession of four spatial images—four surrealistic landscapes—set off and held together by the refrains from the tale of Bluebeard (one of the imprisoned sisters speaks the refrain; the other describes the landscapes). And the implicit meanings of the poem evolve from our awareness of the sisters' dilemma and of the significance of the unfolding landscapes. To put the matter perhaps too bluntly, the sisters may be taken as representatives of human consciousness; the landscapes are images of the cultural waste-land surrounding modern man and of the indifferently brutal but still magnificent world of nature in which man finds himself.

The first landscape and the last present images of a world where only the vestiges of man's culture are apparent; the inter-vening sections present the figure of man dwarfed by his own shadow and unaware of the imprisoned sisters. At the poem's close, after the last anguished cry of the first sister, the second can only reply by disclosing a landscape where the perspective leads but to precipices of emptiness. And these last lines of *Now With His Love* make clear both Bishop's skill as a poet and his sense of modern man's uprootedness and loss of values:

> I see a road. Beyond nowhere
> Defined by cirrus and blue air.
>
> I saw a man but he is gone
> His shadow gone into the sun.

III Minute Particulars

The two features of Bishop's 1935 volume of verse, *Minute Particulars* (the title and title-page epigraph for the book are taken over from William Blake's *Jerusalem*: "He who would do good to another / Must do it in minute particulars"), which distinguish it from its predecessor are a decisive emphasis upon regularly structured verse forms and the appearance of new thematic groupings. These groupings reflect Bishop's newly awakened concern with American culture and his increasing awareness of the contrasts between ancient myth and the con-flicting values of ascetic Christianity and modern science. Echoes from other poets resound too distinctly in some of the poems, but *Minute Particulars* shows Bishop's increasing ability to absorb and transform the influences to which he was always receptive— and also his increasing mastery of an idiom markedly his own.

In preparing his *Selected Poems,* Bishop dropped several of the poems in *Minute Particulars* not pertinent to the 1935 volume's dominant themes; it seems, though, that he excluded them after a consideration of their esthetic merit. "Poor Tom's Song," for example, is too obviously an imitation of Yeats's "Crazy Jane" songs; and "All's Brave that Youth Mounts" is mainly of interest because it shows him working with a verse structure frequently employed in *Minute Particulars*: short lines of two and three stresses, with no definite syllabic count, the accents falling in a pattern that is only loosely iambic, and with the lines held together by irregular and frequently unassertive rhymes:

> I like young men
> Prompt to destroy,
> Resentful youth
> And prodigal boy,
> Pricking such life
> In recalcitrant loins
> They are careless of all
> Embittered coins.

Such a structure is apt to lead to syntactic density, and perhaps to linguistic obscurity of an unwanted sort. In "A Defense" the over-all meaning is fairly obvious, but the poem is unnecessarily clouded in its individual parts. "Metamorphosis," one of Bishop's many poems in praise of sensual love, is an excellent poem through the first five stanzas; then, in the last two stanzas, the speaker too insistently speaks of time's ultimate metamorphosis and too awkwardly turns aside to address the lovers who succeed him.

Of the two non-thematically integrated poems in *Minute Particulars* which Bishop did include in the *Selected Poems*, "Apparition" is the slighter; it is, however, a poem which shows how well Bishop could manipulate the melodic and image-making properties of language. A very personal poem, growing out of his memories of the bird-watching days of his boyhood, the three quatrains re-create the experience of moving through the "pallid light of an undersea day" in a Virginia forest. Employing a line which shifts from the iambic to the trochaic, the poem achieves its effects largely through the use of poetic figures which are reinforced by the subtle use of assonance and alliteration:

> What was it then I saw? Flashing sea-scale,
> Flicker of tail? Sea-bud, sunlight or syren
> Smiling, which even in a boy might move
> Felicity, or failing scatter foam as hail.

If the poem ended here, at the second stanza, it would be too cloying in its beauty; but the last stanza shifts from the dominant sibilants and high-pitched vowels to end on a note of more earthly beauty:

> What did I then? Rose, swam or sank.
> The end was moss. Around me April chuckled,
> The catbird cried upon a dogwood bough,
> And day came crashing through pale judas-bud.

The elegiac poem, "Counsel of Grief," is one in which Bishop is fully in command of the short-lined, irregularly stressed verse structure so frequently employed in *Minute Particulars*. It is very likely that Yeats's use of a roughly similar form in part III of "The Tower" and in several of the pieces in *Words For Music Perhaps,* along with Valéry's example in such works as "Cantique des Colonnes," had a part in Bishop's choice of such a structure. Bishop, however, does not employ rhyme so strictly as the two other poets; and he is not so apt to form his verses into regular stanzaic patterns. "Counsel of Grief" is composed of three sections. The first, addressing a parent who has lost a son, makes use of one of Bishop's favorite image clusters to suggest the nature of the parent's grief: ancient statues still standing above the shards of toppled columns; the second section addresses itself to the dead son, praising his strong delight in living and asking: "How then will you consent, / Being dead, to that dearth / With which the dead are used?"; the third section, then, very skillfully addresses both the grieving parent and the dead youth. The last stanza, which well expresses Bishop's belief that human courage and sympathy might in some measure successfully confront the fact of death, also reveals how well he could handle shifting accents and a tightly packed syntax:

> Assume your dignity,
> And in that silence
> Beyond experience
> Of all our loneliness,
> Smile! It is a lonely
> Mirth the dead have.
> But theirs is the only
> Smile risks never to be less
> Whose fortune is the grave.

Three poems in *Minute Particulars* deal with a theme dominant in *Now With His Love*: the purpose and function of human culture. All three are heavily sexual in their overtones, and at least two are excellent examples of iconic verse. "A Frieze" is both an evocation of antique sculpture (perhaps the frieze referred to is that of the equestrian procession on the Parthenon) and a paean to art. Although "A Frieze" exhibits the most irregular verse structure of all the pieces in the volume, it is neatly divided into two equal parts. The first section presents man's awareness of time's relentless passage—an awareness somehow keyed by sexual passion—by means of an indirect analogy between the dynamic stasis of the sculpture and the sudden insight which overtakes the human animal:

> Arrested like marble horses
> In timeless prancing: in the heave of haunches
> A pause in the prancing:
> Arrested like marble horses, spurred
> By impetuous riders, by furious young heels
> In a tumultuous curve of haunches.

The marble horses, their riders, and the plunging lovers are alike in that they constitute a triumph over time: "Confounding seasons, / To the despair of Apollo." The second section, however, considers that the motion of the statues is fixed and that the lovers' fury must abate. Paradoxically, this second level of awareness only incenses desire and floods the body

> With thoughts that exult though the body tire
> Appeased but afflicted
> With a pain of dissolute longing
> Saved from dilivium of timelessness.

The poem concludes by asking: "Whence comes / This rage?" and by then incorporating the human rage within the metaphor of the sculptured horsemen:

> Dimensionless and undiminishable
> Lust of the timeless prancing, pause in the proud prancing,
> Spurred by the furious heels of immortal horsemen?

The poem, properly, does not answer directly the questions posed; but the answer would seem to be that the "rage," mortal but also "dimensionless and undiminishable," comes both from man's unique sense of himself as an animal bound to time and from his proud knowledge of man's artistic capacity: his ability to arrest time's flux within the forms of art, to give shape and meaning to the "pain of dissolute longing / Saved from diluvium of timelessness."

Another poem celebrating the artist's ability to bring order into human experience—to *fix* and *arrest*, within a meaningful pattern, the disorder of man's animal existence—is "Your Chase Had a Beast in View." It also has a two-part structure, with the second part providing a resolution to the tensions established in the first. This first section, which proceeds through nearly eight of the nine quatrains, describes in language colorful as a medieval tapestry the protracted chase and eventual slaughter of a band of leopards. For the purposes of the poem, it is not necessary that the hunt be looked upon as a symbolic action, but one should keep in mind that the hunters and the hunted sometimes seem to change sides ("luxurious / Leopards in the forest slid. / At times it seemed they hunted us"); and there certainly seem to be sexual overtones hovering about the drawn-out chase and the curious and fluid attraction between beasts and hunters. When the slaughter eventually takes place at the appointed hour, the hunters are momentarily intoxicated by the flowing blood: "Our lives / Exultant spurted in the flood, / A moment young."

At this point, however, "the sweet destruction of / Those spotted beasts" threatens to devolve into nonsensical horror; it is only when the youngest hunter breaks the silence by singing a "stranger love" that the slaughter is redeemed from the accidents of time. By converting the action of the hunt into song, the artist-hunter is able to fix the fluid events of the chase and to give permanence to the brief moment of exultation. The last stanza does not outline for us the hunter's song, but it does symbolically project Bishop's view of the life-enhancing function of art:

> Only in singing it might be
> Supported by the sense alone,
> One syllable of ecstasy
> Confusing shame, confounding bone.

"A Recollection" is one of Bishop's most troublesome poems. partly because the reader unacquainted with the poem's provenance may be unsure about its surface action and partly because one cannot be sure of the function of the vigorously obscene injunction discoverable in the initial letters of the sonnet's fourteen lines (the acrostic is doubly hidden in the *Collected Poems,* where the poem continues from the front to the back of the same leaf). This poem was originally part of the unpublished *The Huntsmen Are Up In America.* In the novel, young Brakespeare inscribes the sonnet on a board fence (a fact that lends a certain appropriateness to the acrostic message) after he has happened upon a portrait of a seventeenth-century Venetian courtesan and is for the first time given a hint of feminine beauty. He is so moved by the portrait that he decides to become a poet, and the sonnet represents the first fruits of his budding genius.

Removed from the confines of the novel, "A Recollection" may be read as a partly iconic poem which praises both sensual beauty and the artistic prowess which, in transmuting that beauty, has made it resistant to the passage of time. The last three lines of the poem make explicit the homage which man owes to beauty—to beauty of being and to the more potent beauty of man's art: "All loveliness demands our courtesies. / Since she was dead I praised her as I could / Silently, among the Barberini bees."

The poem is exceptional both for its fluent command of an ordered structure and for its careful orchestration of verbal music, and it may be that the acrostic message functions as a vigorous counterpoint to the poem's soft subtleties—adding a necessary coarseness and pointing up the essential physicality of the beauty which has given rise to painting and poem alike. The blatant and slangy directive may also be taken as a scornful rejection of all those who belittle the claims of beauty and art; the poem meets the philistine on his own ground and shoves him roughly aside, while it simultaneously exhibits that beauty which the vulgar fail to detect amid the murmur of "the Barberini bees."

If "A Recollection" is a covert attack upon the blindness and vulgarity of the modern world, poems such as "O, Let Not Virtue Seek" and "Night and Day" more openly express Bishop's distaste for the muck of contemporary civilization. While neither is among Bishop's best, both are of significance as attempts to embody some of his central convictions. "Night and Day," a two-part poem, collapses because the images of desolation in part one are not particularly well chosen and because part two does nothing but declaim upon the situation outlined in part one. Although its emphatic rhetoric is not impressive, it does make clear Bishop's disgust with what he deems modern man's servitude to machines: "And the end what? / More speed, more hunger."

"O, Let Not Virtue Seek," one of Bishop's most ambitious efforts, might very well be taken as his response to *The Bridge*, particularly to Section IV, "Cape Hatteras," of Hart Crane's attempted epic. It even seems that Bishop, in matters of verse structure and formal strategy, may have been guided by Crane's example. The thrust of Bishop's poem, though, moves at an angle opposite to that of the other poet. Though there is within Crane's poem a sense of the terrible potential lurking within machines, he struggles to call down a benediction upon man's efforts to break his bondage to earth and by means of science to scale the vaults of space. Crane's airman has within him "a Sanskrit charge / To conjugate infinity's dim marge— / Anew . . .!" And, near the close of "Cape Hatteras," man's space-defying machines are celebrated as the instruments capable of redeeming Walt Whitman's cosmic vision:

> And now, as launched in abysmal cupolas of space,
> Toward endless terminals, Easters of speeding light—
> Vast engines outward veering with seraphic grace
> On clarion cylinders pass out of sight
> To course that span of consciousness thou'st named
> The Open Road—thy vision is reclaimed.

As poetry, "O, Let Not Virtue Seek" is not the equal of "Cape Hatteras" mainly because the irregular verse structure is stiffly handled and because Bishop fails to utilize well the stately diction he employs in the poem; he made extensive revisions before reprinting it in the *Selected Poems,* but the revised version is not much of an improvement. But perhaps it is most important to note that Bishop refuses to go along with Crane's effort to apotheosize man's scientific endeavors. After a series of addresses to aviators and astronomers, the poem concludes by calling down the pilots and by insisting that the astronomers attempt to take the measure of man, doomed and earthbound, but nevertheless glorious in his mortality:

Now take
The height and shadow of our man, our noble
Coriolanus, who still armors the earth,
Albeit dead and never but a man,
And tell us once again what stature his
And what his stride, who nothing asked
Even of a god but his eternity.

Although "O, Let Not Virtue Seek" is not a totally unsatisfactory poem, Bishop's abhorrence of modern man's pride in his imagined conquests of time and space is more effectively rendered in a series of poems that focus upon the landscape and cultural climate of New England and upon the westward-moving American frontier. Before proceeding to a discussion of these poems, however, it is advisable to note that in them, and in most of the poems to be discussed, Bishop set himself the task of achieving a *persona* capable of commenting directly upon the symbolic action of the poem.

As he matured, Bishop tended to abandon the poem of pure symbolic form; his poems increasingly approached the rhetorical and discursive. At about the time of publication of *Minute Particulars*, he wrote Tate: "I am trying to make more and more *statements*, without giving up all that we have gained since Rimbaud." Tate remarks that in these poems "The statement is form" and the legacy of Rimbaud is "the enrichment of language" that modern poets turn to in an effort to mask their uncertainty about form.[23] But Tate is not entirely correct when he says that in Bishop's case the statement provides the form of the poem. Most of his poems have a formal dimension apart from the statements they make; the statements proceed from the form—from the symbolic actions which the poems embody. When Bishop is successful in these later poems, as he very often is, he is able to fuse symbolic action, emotionally charged language, and rhetorical statement into a satisfying whole. And, for the most part, he is successful because he has been able to construct a poetic *persona*, one at the same time involved in and sufficiently apart from the fabric of the poem, which manages, primarily because of the effective language with which Bishop invests his utterances, to shape—without distraction—the reader's response to the symbolic landscape and action of the poem. The task which Bishop set himself was a tricky one, and "O, Let Not

Virtue Seek" demonstrates how he could fall short of his goal;
but many other poems demonstrate that he could hold to the
legacy of the symbolists while breathing new life into poetry of
rhetorical statement.

The five poems brought together in *Minute Particulars* under
the heading "New England" are only loosely related, and some
of them are perhaps weakened by merely autobiographical allusions lost on the reader unacquainted with the details of Bishop's
life. They do, however, possess a certain unity in that they project
images of a desolate landscape rendered even uglier by man's
intrusion upon it, a landscape which is the counterpart of the
despairing and ugly men who inhabit it. The New England of
the poems is a country of "Dishonored houses, / Decaying farm-
lands," a land blighted by the chill ghosts of dead Puritans:

> A hillside shows its jagged teeth
> And white the headstones fall askew.
> Winter not passion sleeps beneath
> The snowy names of Pettigrew.

It is a land where the forlornness of nature is matched by the
bleak disorder of civilization:

> The wilderness comes to the verge
> Of cinders in this chimney'd town,
> And snow and Fords and rust-tins merge
> In hollows where the rain is brown.

In this land, only the forces of nature possess any vitality, but
when spring comes its emblems are ugly ("Yellow troutlilies,
green skunk-cabbage"), and the animals in the woods are murderous. Nature mirrors man's angry futility, and the group of
poems concludes by collocating images of the natural and
civilized worlds to convey a sense of the empty terror which
Bishop saw enveloping America in the 1930's:

> The newspapers brought reports of strikes: shootings,
> Heads broken, or unbandaged led to crime.
> Night, unseen snow in woods, the hungry fox
> Paused, lifted his paw into the scentless wind.

> This was that time, season of crimes and wrath.

Because the five poems in the "New England" sequence are only loosely linked and have little thematic development as the poems unfold, the set should probably not be looked upon as a multi-part but integrated poem of the sort so many modern poets have attempted. The four-part "Experience in the West" is such a poem, and in it Bishop shows how well he could handle the form—even though he came to it rather late in his career. Expert in its modulation of verse structure and striking in its vivid pictorialism, the sequence symbolically projects Bishop's dissenting views about the American pioneer's relentless quest for new frontiers, views which he also set forth in such essays as "The Missing All."[24]

Although "Experience in the West" seems at first glance obscure, most of its difficulties may be resolved by a look at some of Bishop's essays; or, better yet, one may approach it by means of another poem in *Minute Particulars*: the shorter and more straightforward "Southern Pines." The four stanzas of this poem outline a four-stage invasion of the Southern pine forest. The first settlers, "fearing the forest" and "afraid of shadow," savagely scratch out clearings in the woods. The second wave, "tarheels" who slash the pines for the resin, is oblivious to the ugly scars left in its wake. The third wave is that of the lumbermen with "aching pockets"; even more avaricious and thoughtless than the men who preceded them, the timber merchants build shanty boom towns and leave behind them "piny barrens" patrolled by buzzards—symbols of their rapaciousness and brutality. In the fourth stanza, the sharecroppers move in, accompanied by gaunt cattle which attempt to derive sustenance from the cut-over second growth. Apart from providing a compelling image of the destruction which man wrought as he cultivated the frontier, the final stanza is notable as an example of the taut compression characteristic of Bishop's mature verse:

> Cut pine, burnt pine,
> The fourth man's eyes burned in starvation.
> Bone-back cattle, razor-back hogs
> Achieve the seedling, end the pine-woods.

The progression within the four sections of "Experience in the West" is not so orderly as that of the four stanzas of "Southern Pines," but there is the same movement toward sterility and desolation. The first section, "The Burning Wheel," compares the pioneer settlers of America to the Trojans who fled westward under the leadership of Aeneas. These new Trojans have before them a "happy, brave and vast adventure," and for a while their adventure is guided and brightened by the culture which they carry with them, as Aeneas bore Anchises upon his shoulders:

> They, too, the stalwart conquerors of space,
> Each on his shoulders wore a wise delirium
> Of memory and age: ghostly embrace
> Of fathers slanted toward a westward tomb.

After the passing of centuries, however, the ghostly burdens of culture become "light as autumn / Shells of locusts"; the first section concludes by asking: "Where then were they laid? / And in what wilderness oblivion?" The second section, ironically titled "Green Centuries," depicts the forest wilderness in which the pioneer lost both his culture and his soul, where "the New England idea" grudgingly praised in "The Missing All" went sour and was replaced by no viable ideal: "In green no soul was found, / In that green savage clime / Such ignorance of time."

In the wilderness, where "every day dawned Now," the pioneer turned from the recognition of the past to inordinate dreams of conquering space: "Time dreams eternity. / Their nights were starred with space." In the present, however, now that the conquest of the continent has been attained, the pioneer's vision is clouded and bereft of meaning:

> But now an idle frown
> Compels the death-set face,
> Where dwindled to a glaze
> Angers an old hawk's gaze.

The third section, "Loss in the West," further explores the fate of the frontiersman and his now-outmoded virtues, virtues which in the present reveal themselves as essentially motivated by a savage hatred of life. After the frontiersman's conquest, only "The vile rattle / Remains"; the wild pigeon is vanished and "slaughtered / The scarlet wattle." Demanding that Americans "Repudiate that blood" and turn away from the man who, with "Time lost," was unable to find himself in "limitless space," the poet depicts the pioneer as damned because he has destroyed his own life in raping nature: "And the blood dried / Coursing about his bones. In another fur / The bright beast died." Although bereft of life, the skeleton figure of the frontiersman still moves restlessly within the American landscape; and "Loss in the West" concludes by wondering about the present object of the quest bequeathed to the modern American by his pioneer ancestor: "What? Wheel of the sun / In heaven? The west wind? Or only a will / To his own destruction?"

The fourth section, "O Pioneers!" (a title even more pointedly ironic than "Green Centuries"), answers the questions posed at the end of "Loss in the West" by presenting surrealistic images of a gold-seeking party lost and perishing in the desert. As the poem unfolds, the speaker simultaneously addresses both the bewildered pioneers and his present audience. "O Pioneers!" is an indictment both of the mad lust of the frontiersman and of the modern American's willingness to glamorize the march across the continent:

> The way is lost to fortune. Forward, back,
> Delirium will never find a stream
> Running gold sands. Rather the earth will crack
> Dry on skeletons, skulls in some daft scheme,
>
> Sockets of eyes that perished crazily,
> Ignorant of sun, the sagebrush, mad
> Even to the dew. A continent they had
> To ravage, and raving romped from sea to sea.

"Experience in the West," eminently successful as poetry, is also notable as a vigorous rejection of the prevailing American myth of the frontier—a subject celebrated in the 1920's and 1930's by such diverse figures as Hart Crane, Carl Sandburg, Archibald MacLeish, and John Steinbeck. In questioning the myth, Bishop is akin to Southern contemporaries such as Faulkner and Warren; but it is important to keep in mind that "Experience in the West" antedates "The Bear" and *World Enough and Time.*

While the "New England" and "Experience in the West" sequences are indicative of Bishop's efforts to grapple with the facts of American culture, he still continued to make poetic capital of his intense love for the Mediterranean. The remaining poems in *Minute Particulars* call into play the antique world which provides so much of the substance of such poems as the "Ode" and "The Return." And these remaining poems tend to fall into two categories into which both "The Return" and the "Ode" might fit: some are poems grounded in the history and historical legends of the Mediterranean basin; others explore the complex mythology of Mediterranean culture. There are at least two good poems in the first group; the second contains some of Bishop's finest and most important poems.

Two of the four "historical" poems deal with the legend of Troy. The lesser, "Hecuba's Rage," contrasts the oblivious love of Paris and Helen with the unspent anger of Hecuba. The poem is aware of the rightness of Hecuba's wrath; but it ends by noting that it is to the lovers we owe the immortal legacy of the legend of Troy: "Because of them those wars remain / And Troy, uncrowned of an old queen." The other, "Farewell to Many Cities," a descant upon the nine successive cities of Troy, questions the permanence of modern civilization. In some ways similar to "The Return," "Farewell" more pointedly calls attention to its underlying analogy by means of a rhetorical question posed in the jarring penultimate stanza (the title of the poem on its first publication, "Return to New York," further called attention to the comparison between present and past). The chief virtue of the poem is its handling of rhyme and movement within the narrowly restricted quatrains:

> Nine sea-cities
> Of Ilion's lineage
> Displaced the seas
> And won great wage
>
> In war. Time counterfeits
> Change. Their Aprils
> Washed violets
> Among white hills.

Complementing the Trojan themes of "Hecuba's Rage" and "A Farewell to Many Cities" are two poems which have as their background the decline of imperial Rome. "An Interlude" is a recasting, longer and not nearly so felicitous, of "The Return." It lacks the earlier poem's compactness and symbolic brilliance; it does, however, gain a certain humorous dimension if one reads it as a wry commentary on the efforts of the New

Deal to cope with the social disorders brought on by the depression of the 1930's.

"No More the Senator," an excellent poem which Mr. Tate says was written as an exhortation to Edmund Wilson "to give up serious political activity and to withdraw into private virtue,"[25] does not have to be construed so narrowly in order for the reader to make out its import. The poem is a dramatic monologue by an ex-senator who has retired into a Christian monastery, but the "virtue" which it celebrates is that of the earthly and precarious domain of art—not that prized by the heaven-oriented new religion. For the old senator, who has seen the image of the true Caesars "only in stone," the regimen of monkly life is not difficult; he finds, however, "It is / The conduct of the mind that's hard to change." The new doctrine he has "conceived with the mind," but the landscape outside his cell is so poignantly beautiful that he cannot let go his love for poetry. The heresy which troubles him is that "Christ did not die for poets," and so he belabors his scribes in an attempt to preserve poetry against the overweening claims of the religion to which he has given his allegiance:

> So I say Hurry!
>   Hurry the Clouds!
>   For Heaven is high
> And cannot hear our comedies. Hurry
> My Seneca and Euripides!
>   For Tragedy stays here.

The poem concludes with a complex image which simultaneously conveys Bishop's awareness of poetry's necessary involvement with earthly time and his high regard for the fragile beauty which poets may bear away from their doomed struggle with time :

>   And I have seen
> The crows feed black when gathered to the grain.
> They also die: poets
> Whose immortality grows by the river bed in reeds.

The most memorable of the "mythological" poems in *Minute Particulars* treat of man's involvement with time and with the earth which gives him sustenance. In addition to these poems, which find their prose counterpart in Bishop's essay on *The*

Golden Bough, there are several other less accomplished poems which make use of mythic material. A variation upon the materials of the great "Ode," "The Mothers" presents chthonian goddesses whose impenetrable meaning is an oppressive weight upon the consciousness of modern man; it lacks, however, the force of the "Ode" and is marred by an uncertainty in the handling of the verse structure. "The Coming of Persephone," one of Bishop's worst poems, is wrecked by cloying sweetness of diction, an overinsistent use of alliteration and assonance, and an absence of subtle control over the short line lengths. More rewarding is "Another Acteon." Worthy of praise for its skilled handling of the modulations within the blank-verse measure, this poem employs the figure of the presumptuous Greek hunter to suggest the confusion and shame of modern man in flight from punishment for crimes for which he stands self-convicted even though he cannot make out their exact nature.

When Bishop assembled his 1941 volume, he put into a separate grouping—along with a later poem about the crucifixion, "Trinity of Crime"—the four remaining poems which have mythology as their axis: "The Sword Dance," "The Tree," "The Saints," and "Divine Nativity." Although composed as early as 1922, "The Sword Dance" fits in with the other poems, and its date of composition reveals that Bishop was attracted very early in his career by the poetic potential within mythology. The poem seems to have grown out of a reading of the seventh chapter of Jessie Weston's *From Ritual to Romance,* the book which provided a foundation for *The Waste Land.* Miss Weston describes several forms of ancient ritualistic sword dances which in her view demonstrate that the Aryan Indians and the ancient Greeks "held the conception of a group of Beings, of mythic origin, represented under the guise of armed youths, who were noted dancers, and whose activities were closely connected with the processes of Nature."[26] Bishop's poem gorgeously presents the dance of such daimonic Beings: "In golden clamor they tread the clouds / Dancing, a burnish of youths—their changing lustres / Move in a tumult of light."

While the poem hints at the relationship between the mythic dance and man's desires "to stimulate the reproductive energies of Nature"[27] ("their pointed swords / Touch to the sound of rain, outdistanced by thunder"), its primary emphasis is upon the gulf which separates the immortal dancers and the mortals who worshipfully witness their unceasing motion. Paradoxically, the poem implies that the lot of man is in some ways preferable to that enjoyed by the youthful immortals. It is the daimons who are "dead, being deathless," even though they are eternally "strong / As we dying are not." Like the figures on Keats's Grecian urn, the divine dancers are arrested in their perpetual motion; they can never experience the fruition of being which man may attain, even though he is destined for death. The brittle imagery of the final stanza of the poem clearly indicates that Bishop prefers man's condition of impermanence to the unceasing whir of the deathless swordsmen:

> They have not dropped their swords; their comeliness
> Is unchanging, their fruitfulness still to garner.
> They turn like one form in a circling abyss of glass
> Reflecting the glittering feet, the less bright armor.

Bishop's celebration of those distinctly human virtues which he felt were discernible in Frazer's unwitting revelation of "the true religion of mankind" are more directly at the center of the oblique symbolism of "The Tree." Making use of motifs drawn from the myth of Adam and Eve, "The Tree" focuses upon the indissoluble relationships between death and human life. The poem begins with the injunction "Return to the tree!" and swiftly describes the approach of Adam and Eve to the tree of Life and its desired but forbidden fruit. The man and woman desire to "touch" the "sun-rimmed fruit," but its promise of life may not be fulfilled until the two accept the death which it also bodes: "But the touch denied / Until embraced / By the lips with death's taste." When the fruit is finally accepted, they become human and are caught up by sexual desire: "a bright / Burnish of desire / Bordering all their tree with fire." In becoming human and consequently bound over to death, the two have lost their divine status; but they have simultaneously been brought into such closeness with the processes of nature that they now seem to be more truly masters of life than they were before:

> From the living stem
> Such sustenance
> Draws into their dance
> Stars follow them.
> Clasping they control
> The coursing light from pole to pole.

The poem concludes with two stanzas which continue to underline the inseparable bonds between passionate life and inexorable death. There is terror in the final stanza that pictures the transformation of the forbidden fruit to the corpse of the hanged Vegetation God—"There where all the planets sang / See him a destroyer hang!"—but the poem refuses to waver in the presence of the terror. It bravely calls upon men and women to illumine their lives with a passion which will redeem the deaths they must experience:

> Let them fructify
> Their tree of death!
> With brute breath
> Let them die!
> All delight of leaf and sun
> Dreams of dissolution.

"The Tree" needs to be read in conjunction with "The Saints," which explores the consequences of man's efforts to deny his "brute breath" and to escape the bondage of earthly time. The speaker of this poem surveys a group of ascetic hermits, "starvelings" who have abandoned the shores of the Mediterranean and fled into the African desert in an effort to subdue their bodily passions. They are in love with death, but their skeleton embrace of death is not akin to the acceptance which Bishop praises in *"The Golden Bough"*; it is not the "acceptance of death as fulfillment which comes to strong men when life is at the full." Instead, they are in love with non-being, possessed by a desire similar to that which Bishop discerned in medieval church music and Byzantine frescoes: "what speaks from that music is nothing so strong as the will to die, but merely a desire not to be. It is this desire and no other which looks out at us from the will-less and . . . soulless eyes of Byzantine saints" (*CE*, 29-30). In their effort to escape from history, the ascetics are similar to the pioneers of "Experience in the West"; but, whereas the desert imagery of the former poem is employed to suggest the madness of the pioneer's attempts to conquer space, the burning sun and windblown sand of "The Saints" underline the futility of all efforts to negate the senses and to attain "divinity" outside time.

The first of the poem's five sections, all of which make use of the short line lengths and irregular rhymes so frequently encountered in *Minute Particulars*, describes the "starvelings" as they endure the fire of the desert sun. Their lips are "Shrivelled black," and they are so emaciated that one can make out "on ribs unfleshed / The heartbeat bare." Facing the "void" of the sky, "Dark eyes were burnt / To great holes that saw / Visions that were not / Africa." Section one hints at the motives of the would-be saints: "As who would say / All that has age / We must wither away!"; section two further dramatizes their rage against the natural order of growth and decay. Having witnessed the collapse of the Roman Empire, they cry out: "Let us stretch / To the scorpion / This dying itch of generation." Angry against the fact of their birth, they attempt to deny their mortality:

> Subduing time
> In naked trance,
> Construe as crime
> Continuance,
> All that changes
> Confound with scorn.
> So each man avenges
> A child born.

In the short third section, the speaker stresses the reasons which make impossible the saints' effort to purge away their humanity and to attain a state of being not subject to time's ravages; in his view, "The gods alone / Know not age, or the grave," and "Only endures / The unchanging god."

Bishop felt that man could attain his proper divinity only by admitting his doom and by living to the fullest the short span of life granted him. The final two sections of "The Saints" meditate upon the essential wrongness and the tragic cost of the ascetic vision. The saints' prayer is "Dilate / Our loves beyond / All loves that age / Or lust consumes"; but the speaker of the poem insists that "Whoever says / Divine has said / Dying" and that "Always / Is a word for the dead." The life-denying hermits are maddened by a rage that has no attainable end:

> So that dying thinned
> In an alien land,
> Wrapped by the wind
> In mummying sand,
> Can but mitigate
> Excess of breath,
> While we await
> The god in death.

The final section of the poem—in which the speaker notes that he is "haunted by / Silence in the sun, / An African eye / Singed by its vision"—testifies both to the potent temptation inherent in the ascetic vision and to the prevalence of such longings in the modern world, longings to break away from the natural round of awaiting "The god in death." The poem concludes, however, with a warning assessment of the costs of such anti-human visions and longings:

> Saints can commit
> Burning excess
> In the thorn thicket
> Of the sun's wilderness,
> At divine cost
> Thinned to a breath
> That the wind can exhaust
> In the sun's wrath.

"Divine Nativity," the poem at the end of *Minute Particulars,* is similar to "The Sword Dance" in that it considers man's mythic figuration of the divine in the shape of the deities to whom he gives his worship: more specifically, it is concerned with the descent of the gods to men and their assumption of natural forms to reveal themselves to man. Bishop treats both pagan and Christian myth, implying that all myths contain a "fabled truth" which has as its center an insistence upon the human need to fuse divine aspiration and sensuous passion. In each of the poem's five sections, the divine is made manifest only when it is attended by an access of sexuality. In the first two sections, the sexual dimensions of the Christian myth of the Incarnation are suggested by such lines as "A god is conceived / In a revel of thighs" and "But a god is born / Of a body's gash / To an old man's scorn / In pain." The third and fourth sections, which take up pagan mythology, emphasize the sexuality connected with the gods' appearances by moving from the myths in which the gods assume human guises to those in which they take on theriomorphic shape:

> Adoring Leda leaned upon
> A bright encumbrance of wild swan.
> Europa rode rejoiced through all
> The wild romp of briny bull.

In the final section, pagan and Christian myth coalesce, and Bishop praises them equally as embodiments of the human understanding which has created them as a means of expressing the deep-felt need to unite both the physical and the spiritual impulses within man:

> Eagle, swan or dove,
> White bull or cloud,
> Incarnate love
> Alone is proud.
> The arrogant know
> In the bestial part
> Overflow
> Of the elated heart.

As Joseph Frank has noted in discussing "The Tree," "The Saints," and "Divine Nativity," Bishop resembles D. H. Lawrence "in his emphasis on sexuality and his rejection of asceticism." But he differs from Lawrence in that he does not "simply surrender to the deification of the primitive and chthonic powers." Bishop emphasizes the sensuous, "the bestial part," in order to realize an "overflow" in the intellectual and spiritual component of man, "the elated heart." In his move toward a sensuous humanism, Bishop closely resembles Wallace Stevens. In the long run, however, Stevens' humanism is curiously inhuman and remote, while Bishop maintains throughout his verse a vitality equally composed of passion and intelligence. The case for Bishop is well put by Joseph Frank when he says: "the fine balance of Bishop's humanism, expressed in the firm control of these masterly poems, seems to me to entitle them to a distinguished place in contemporary poetry."[28]

IV   *The Poetry of Bishop's Final Years*

Preceding sections of this chapter have dealt at length with most of the poems in *Now With His Love* and *Minute Particulars*. In this final section, detailed consideration will be given only a few of the poems Bishop wrote in the last years of his life. Such a procedure is justifiable because, as Frank observes, most of the sixteen new pieces included in the 1941 *Selected Poems* "do not reveal any significant development in Bishop's works; only his accustomed mastery in familiar themes and styles."[29] A similar judgment may be pronounced on most of the uncollected and unpublished poems of Bishop's final years. One should not pass too swiftly over these poems, however, for Bishop's "mastery" is unfalteringly displayed in several of them. In addition, the very fact that in them he returns to already established themes points up the continuity and wholeness of Bishop's mature verse. In glancing briefly at these poems, the emphasis will be upon the thematic links among them and with the earlier verse. For convenience's sake, the poems Bishop saw in print and those unpublished during his lifetime will be considered separately.

Several of Bishop's later poems turn upon the celebration of sensual love. "Invitation at Dawn," an amorous aubade, enlists lovers under the sign of Venus and figures love as a contest with time: "All time contending / and our love unending." Even more sensual is another "dawn" poem, "Les Balcons qui Rêvent," which incorporates phallicism and mythic overtones to suggest the life-enhancing function of sexuality:

> Rustling a green of paradise
> The light reflects her opened eyes;
> And laughter sees the antique snake
> Resume the aspect of a god.

More oblique in their homage to sensuality are "The Spare Quilt" and "The Submarine Bed," two poems which indirectly contrast the passionless puritanism and cold decrepitude of New England with youthful vitality and splendor. The old couple of "The Spare Quilt" must make do with dreams of "young / Indulgent hunters" while they "stitch the cold night out," and the nightgowned couple who come together in "The Submarine Bed" discover that after their effort to dissociate themselves from the act of lust "It is not easy to adjust / The body to a severed head."

Somewhat similar to the poems in praise of sensual love are several which honor youth and heroic action. Among these—most of which take their controlling images from ancient myth and history—are "Phaeton," "Why They Waged War," "Whom the Gods Love," "A Charm," and "The Parallel." Worthy of notice because of its careful use of the sea and sand imagery so characteristic of Bishop's later verse, "The Parallel" is one of Bishop's most skillfully wrought poems. Employing fairly exact rhyme and meter, it moves swiftly from the opening landscape of sea and sand toward an evocation of Antony at the crisis of Actium.

The concluding rhetorical statement which declares Antony's heroic stature has been well prepared for by the preceding portions of the poem.

Another set of poems, not so closely related as those in the two groupings outlined above, may be viewed as having as a central theme the collapse and aimlessness of modern culture. "Occupation of a City," which suggests the take-over of Paris by the Germans, depicts the silence of a city being overwhelmed by the "armor of a depraved glory." "Collapse of Time" provides further images of the American physical and social landscape disfigured by technological greed and civic disorder. In "The 'Yankee Trader'" an old sofa abandoned in the snow outside an antique shop functions both as a symbol of discarded cultural values and as emblem of the possible continuance of the civilized virtues it once embodied. Another "New England" poem, however, "Ghouls' Wharf," proposes little hope for modern culture. The old man who sees in the waves tossing on the wharf the damned souls of his fellow men believes that he might have evoked different images from the sea, but concludes that such images would have been of no avail to himself or to others as lost and chilled as he:

> "I might have called up sea-blue crowds
> Or gods that scale from green to bronze.
> But what should I do, old man, with gods
> Whose glory to their guilt responds?"

Several of Bishop's last published poems were prompted by memories of his childhood and by reflections upon his ancestry. "Fourteen" is a look back at his adolescent delight in ornithology, and "Interior" is based upon his youthful memories of the quiet richness of a Southern parlor. "Conquest of the Wind" is quite similar to "Beyond Connecticut, Beyond the Sea" in its evocation of his forebears. In the later poem, however, Bishop repudiates his ancestors. He sees them as having participated in the frontier march and regrets that his "long since born and now abandoned bones / Are scattered, white dust, about this continent." In the poem, his kinsmen are lost among the westward-trekking pioneers; unable to take pride in "The triumph of that space destroying rage," he turns to the earth and to all its dead in an effort to establish continuity and a place in time:

Our past is in the ground and not the blood.
Descended from the generations of those graves.
Let me a little while pluck a green pride
Before the lightning burns the stricken leaves.

Two of the late poems, "That Summer's End" and "The Dream,"
invite psychoanalytical interpretations which would revolve about
the illness Bishop experienced after his father's death and his
mother's remarriage. Only "The Dream," however, possesses
merit as poetry; it may stand alone as a poem about the terrors
possibly involved in any effort to realize the truth about the
past. Tightly controlled in its verse, the poem projects both the
hallucinatory quality of nightmare and the chilling finality of
self-knowledge—along with a loving acceptance of human frailty
and human passion.

Many of the poems remaining unpublished at the time of
Bishop's death are slight, and many are of interest mainly
because they probe themes and essay modes more successfully
realized in other poems. Several are first-rate, however, and even
some of the slightest display the keenness and depth of his poetic
imagination. His ability to make fresh the epigrammatic mode is
evident not only in "Three Days" and "Eros," which appear in
the *Selected Poems*, but in such unpublished poems as "The
Promise," "Poem of Four Lines With Three Titles," "A Small
Thing," and "A Dedication."[30] Several of the unpublished efforts
reveal Bishop's earthy humor, the touch of coarseness which
strengthened his elegance and gave vigor to his sensuality. Poems
of this sort worthy of separate notice are the bawdy "Radio City,"
(SR), the self-caricaturing "Epitaph for a Poet," the purposely
vulgar "Percy Shelley," and the untitled two-stanza poem which
pokes fun at the postures indulged in by liberal thinkers of
the 1930's:

You'd think that he would cause a shock
The scorpion with his double cock,
Both sides erect, but not at all.
The scorpion is a liberal.

One thrusts to right, one sticks to left
As he advances toward the cleft
And then presents in copulation
The New Republic of the Nation

Although generally the unpublished pieces are not so successfully executed as the late published poems, one can see in them,
early and late, Bishop adumbrating and returning to themes
characteristic of his mature verse. The late "Nativity," a Yeats-
echoing poem having as its subject the birth of Christ, has its
kinship with the "Divine Nativity" sequence; "Let Apollo's favorite tree . . ." (SR) is similar to "The Tree" in its injunction to
man to accept the double facts of sexuality and mortality. "The
Emperor Also Was a God" deals with the disintegrating Roman
Empire envisioned in "The Return" and "An Interlude," and the
early "Baroque" introduces the two desert Antonies who figure
in such poems as "The Parallel" and "The Saints." "Four Noble
Horses," an iconic poem describing the bronze statues atop
San Marco in Venice, is very similar in theme and imagery to
"A Frieze," and "A Green and Pleasant Land" anticipates "Southern Pines" and "Collapse of Time." Another poem which incorporates Bishop's love of art and his distrust of modern science is
the semi-iconic "Paolo Uccello's Battle Horses," which concludes
by contrasting the lasting strength of art with the desolation
brought on by scientific speculation: "Now Einstein's head is
wearier than age; / Night dies; and sun alone the morning
proves. / But dawn shall hear those mighty buttocks praised."

Apart from "The Statues" sequence, discussed at length later
on in this section, the most impressive among Bishop's late unpublished poems are the "Meaning of a Lion," "The Boy Alone,"
and "The Bull Is Time." In its focus upon sheer animality, the
"Meaning of a Lion" is unique among Bishop's humanistically
oriented verse. The unstated burden of the poem is that the
lion's appetites are inhuman and that he is neither bothered nor
blessed by human desires. Wholly united with nature and time,
the lion, when he dies, "rots without remorse." To a certain
extent, the lion is an image of positive virtue, for he enjoys the
"Tall curvet of immortal lust" and is at home within the desert
which, in "The Saints," mocks at human desires. The imagery of
the poem, however, underlines the brutality and senselessness of
the short life enjoyed by the lion.

"The Boy Alone" (SR) focuses upon the human awareness of
time and its passing which the brute neither knows nor suffers.
One of the poems in which Bishop most masterfully employs his
distinctive verse structure of short-line lengths and approximate
rhymes, "The Boy Alone" makes use of a superior *persona* who

observes and reports upon the process whereby a boy at play upon a beach becomes aware of human mortality. Integrated within the poem are Bishop's characteristic images of sun, sand, and sea; and fully realized within its language and movement are his paired themes of man's tragic consciousness of time and his necessary involvement with the mutual processes of life and death.

"The Bull Is Time" (SR) seems, on the evidence of the many manuscript versions of the poem among the Bishop Papers at Princeton, never to have been finished to his complete satisfaction. Even in the tentative state in which he left it, however, "The Bull Is Time" is an excellent, important poem. In what is probably his last attempt to deal with the artist's effort to "present the conflict of man with time" in order to provide for man "a release from time" (CE, 104), he employs a metaphor of sexual union similar to that at the center of "Speaking of Poetry." In the later poem, however, and probably as a direct consequence of his absorption with mythology, the figures of Europa and the Bull assume the roles previously played by Desdemona and Othello. The speaker of the poem, after first noting that the "desperation" of which he complains is not prompted by his personal fate, stresses the arduousness of his task, the presentation of "that conflict which I wage / Between Europa and the Bull." Europa is femininity and human delicacy; the divine Bull, the embodiment of natural force and the relentless press of time. The poet sees that Europa, in order to receive the embrace of the Bull, must be violated: "I know that he must trample her, / I see her whiteness must be bruised." The movement of the poem, however, makes it clear that the poet's task is not so much a recognition of the necessary union between delicacy and brutality as the ordering of the vision; the poet's duty, one both noble and maddeningly difficult, is to fix and give form to the coupling of the graceful Europa and the awesomely forceful Bull:

> And so they stay
> Suspended while I strive to rhyme
> Furious conflict, the hoofs' play
> And the prone girl. This Bull is Time.

The late poems to be discussed at some length are "Resurrection," "The Statues," "Colloquy with a King-Crab," "A Subject of Sea Change," and "The Hours." All these are major poems, and within them may be seen, complementing each other, the technical mastery of verse which the mature Bishop achieved and the comprehensiveness and depth of his compassionate intelligence.

"Resurrection" is both the culmination of Bishop's persistent grappling with mythological themes and the seeming end of his disillusioned inability to wholly embrace within his mythological schema the figure of Christ. Although his essay on *The Golden Bough* had suggested that Christ could be accepted as one of the host of Vegetation Gods ("But taking religion as a revelation of human destiny, we must see that He is not less divine because of the company of Adonis, Osiris and Thammus. His divinity is to be found in precisely those attributes which He shares with these and older incarnate gods." [*CE*, 28]), most of the 1930's poems in which Christ appears present Him as a meaningless figure who no longer has any import for modern man. In both the "Ode" and "Trinity of Crime," a 1934 poem included among the *Selected Poems*, great emphasis is placed upon the unavailing death and unapproachability of Christ. In "Trinity of Crime," He is merely one of three crucified upon Calvary: "His destiny / Upon a place of skulls is ended. He is dead / And one of three."

"Resurrection," however, is totally different; Christ is seen as humanly divine; and His passion is envisioned as partaking of "the true religion of mankind." It is important to note, however, that the "Resurrection" of which the poem speaks is not the resurrection of a god but the continuity and rebirth of nature—and that the poem deals solely with the death of Christ. In His death, and by virtue of His acceptance of death, the cross on which He hangs becomes imbued with life:

> The tree that had been dead was quick
> Resurgent branches every one
> Broke into green, and air was thick
> With leaves all crowding toward the sun.

In the poem, all of Bishop's ability to create vivid pictorial images is brought into play to suggest the joy emanating from the young God's willing embrace of death:

> Rustling like flames, the leaves went up
> And when the sun came down to gild
> Tree from the ground to glittering top
> Wounds in the hands and feet were healed.

Hardly a "Christian" poem, in the usual sense of the term, "Resurrection" is nevertheless a poem in praise of the mythic figure of Christ: a Christ envisioned as one of a company of young gods who, by virtue of their joyful acceptance of death, reveal to men the necessary dependence of life upon death and the necessary submission of man to the cyclic rhythms of nature. "Trinity of Crime" and "Ode" are joyless and oppressive poems, but there is exuberant release and celebration in "Resurrection." The joy and celebration are not precisely similar to that which Christians are supposed to experience on Easter morning, but they are not vastly different from the emotions appropriate to Christians who delight in the fruits of Christ's sufferings:

> So lucid was that suffering
> In leaves! Of one wound the god died
> And all the undyings of the spring
> Decked from the wound within his side.

Although "Resurrection" may be read as evidence of Bishop's acceptance of the mythic substance of Christianity, the unpublished sequence "The Statues," written at about the same time, makes it clear that his sympathies were still mainly given over to the pagan mythos of the ancient Mediterranean. One of his most successful efforts at combining rhetorical statement with poetically charged language and symbolic density, this group of poems is also notable for its control of a verse structure employing a wide range of line lengths and verbal patterns. Giving unity to the sequence is a complex symbolic design which has as its main elements the contrasting imagery of sea and desert and the interwoven figures of frail human beings and the gods man embodies in statues and temples. Picking up themes from such earlier poems as "The Saints," "Experience in the West," and "The Tree," the sequence is one of Bishop's most ambitious attempts to give poetic voice to his analysis of the woes of modern culture.

In the first section, "The Uneaten Gods," the speaker of the poem, who is presumably standing on the western shores of the Atlantic, contrasts the civilization of which he is part with that of the pagan Mediterranean. Now, the potentially life-giving sea casts up only "broken" images of the gods, and those who wander upon the shore "Cannot eat the bodies of these gods." The ruined gods are unavailing and foreign to modern man because he is heir to "the initial error, the fatal mischief," of not seeing within the processes of nature a genuine divinity: "This was in truth the fatal error. / When food and drink are no more divine / Then they fail, they fail the body."

After a passage in which the speaker emphasizes the extent to which modern man has lost all sense of the mysterious significance of the sea ("Only the waves are seen / Covetous of land, / Not the force under the waves, / Nor the forces above the waves"), the first section concludes with a brilliant passage describing a time when the gods were properly admitted and consequently "restored / Stars to the turning year." The passage stresses two complementary aspects of this past age. First, there was an access of human love: "Therefore, in love / With sun, the lovers clasped, the child was born, / Incarnate marvel of exhausted summer." Second, the arts flourished:

> Imaginings of order
> Rose, beyond the lucent headlands,
> Above the marble stairs. And columns rose,
> Voluptuous doves among the capitals,
> Supporting roof and overcoming azure.

With the proper recognition of the divine forces of nature, man is able to give order to his life, and as long as the images of the gods stood in the temples, "the state / And every sea-gaze circled to the same horizon, / All speech proclaimed one tongue of praise."

In the next two sections, "Dunes on the March" and "Sojourn in the Desert," images of desert waste and sterility supplant those depicting the fecundating sea and the order-bringing statues. These sections, highly reminiscent of "The Saints," make clear the consequences of man's abandonment of the sea-born gods. St. John, who has displaced "Amphion Orpheus" (the two figures from Greek myth symbolize cultural order and sacramental participation in the order of nature), has failed in his search for the incarnate "Word": "His gaze bewildered, / Could not for all his meditation hear it. / It was not in the Wilderness." Gazing upon the wilderness of the present, the speaker can discover only faint traces of the lost Atlantis of the pagan past:

> Surviving shores
> Of a sunken continent: sand and scrub-pine,
> Scrub-oak and sand; the aromatic blaze
> Of a blue noon warms the bay-leaf in the sea's sound.

The "sea's sound" and hints of Atlantis at the close of "Sojourn in the Desert" provide a transition to the next section, "Return of the Sea," where the pounding ocean is not the bringer of life but the relentless embodiment of death. After the barrenness of the desert vision, the speaker welcomes the avenging fury of the sea:

> Grateful the sound of the sea! Destruction cast
> Upon the sterile shingle, grating the shores
> In one white death of spray.

With the pulse of the destroying sea ringing in his ears, the speaker now imaginatively plunges into the depths of the ocean. His impulse is toward death, but the four stages of his "Sounding" bring him back to light again. "Return of the Sea," at the pivotal middle of the poem, may therefore be viewed as the dramatization of a descent into darkness which the *persona* must essay to establish his role as prophet-spokesman and, also, to attain the wisdom with which he speaks.

In the first of the "Sounding" passages, one reminiscent both of Bishop's own "The Return" and of Whitman's "Out of the Cradle Endlessly Rocking," the speaker enjoins himself and his audience to "Return to darkness" and to the water rushing as though it "were the word / Death made flesh / The Word Death / And the Word made flesh!" After this horrifying vision of the Incarnation, the speaker, startled, discovers he is Narcissus, who finds in the "secret pools" of the sea his "own remorseless face" amid "strange starfish and salt-oozing weed!" In the next passage the depths of the sea become, in words from Valéry which Bishop quoted in his 1941 address on "The Arts in America," "the profound depths of history."[31] Through these sunken currents the speaker sees gliding the once-fabled ships of vanished civilizations: "prows that darkly clove / Oncoming crests while they pursued / Their gilded course toward the untrafficked isles." Then, after the disillusioning visions of self and history, follows the final injunction: to set forth into the midst of the seas. In this passage, subtly reminiscent of Crane's "Voyages," there are mingled both suicidal longings and a vision of a return to breath and light; the section ends by re-asserting the continuity of life:

> Sounding
> Swim
> And let your naked breath expire
> Under the overwhelming onslaught of the sea,
> Or crook with counterstroke the coming wave
> And rise, turned on a breath, and see
> The sun in conscious triumph on the sky!

Just as the "sea's sound" at the end of "Sojourn in the Desert" provides a bridge to "Return of the Sea," so the sun triumphant in the sky leads the reader forward to the next section, "The Statues of Shadow." Returned, alive, to the sandy Atlantic coast, the speaker is nevertheless frightened by the "mystery of clearest light" in which he stands and by his shadow projected by the sun: "I saw my body cast / In shadow and was afraid." He is also frightened by his awareness of time: "I saw time vast / As my own shadow and was afraid." Illuminated by the sun, however, he is suddenly aware of his own presence as a human being; and his shadow consequently becomes a "stature." With this knowledge, the oppressive past which weighs upon him (the life-denying interlude depicted in "Dunes on the March" and "Sojourn in the Desert") becomes no more significant than his own shadow. Such a vision entails responsibility, but it no longer carries with it the taste of fear:

> The shade of all those centuries
> Whose death is longing and fate a crime
> Lay long
> But no longer
> Than the statue of shadow
> The sun at its silent noon laid at my feet.

After the descent into the sea and the encounter with the shadow, the speaker is prepared, in the final sections of the sequence, to evoke once more those ancient cultures which in the past properly recognized the divine lineaments of nature—and finally to celebrate that wholehearted acceptance of life and death which Bishop deemed proper for man.

In "The Great Statues," the *persona* for the first time speaks directly to the poem's audience, engaging both himself and his hearers to "sustain the silence of great statues / Who stare out it seems in appalled serenity." Such statues are doomed to crumble, but only with the slow deliberateness of "rage wearing down rock / Ancient as the dawn." In a passage reminiscent of "Experience in the West," the speaker announces that he has "awakened from a dream of space" and that he has forever departed from the land where there is "No saying of the Sun / That does not say Cease, cease!" After once again urging himself and his audience to "stay by these ancient statues," which remind men that "the gods were once beasts," he concludes by remarking that the statues may speak to man in his present fear, may remind him that

> Not death
> Is the last indignity of man, but an endless
> Dying. Time lost, and centuries uncounted,
> Violence reverberating under the arches,
> The land dead and all wars disastrous.

In the final section, the speaker, still standing on the shores of the Atlantic, recognizes that the antique past is perhaps irrecoverable. He nevertheless insists that the natural order which once gave birth to the gods is unchangingly constant and thus still capable of firing man's imagination:

> The day returns, but not the day
> Of these gods. Yet the dawn resumes the amazed
> Smile of a brute Apollo,
> Dazzling in bronze of sea-encrusted blue-green.

Still bedazzled by images of isles where "temples erect their solitudes / Columns and white porches aloft in stone / The eyeless statues of corrupted gods," the speaker also knows that the once-brilliant noon of the statue-gods is now "descended / Into solid bodies on the beach, / With the sun burning, darkened / And burning with blood." Watching the "laughter-running boys" on the beach, who are now the best avatars of the departed gods, "Leap, and maintain their increase in the air," the speaker utters these lines witnessing his acceptance of man's limited but potentially noble place in nature:

I was twice born,
Once begotten by my father,
Once by the divine Sun,
My will consenting to that Word whose will
Ordains the copulations and the putrefactions,
The seed dying that love may not die,
The death of seed that the body may not die,
Corruption of the body that the land may not perish.

After this swelling declaration of faith, the closing, diminu-
endo, passages of "The Archipelagoes" move through a last
invocation of the sea (which is "formless" but capable of
"wreathing all the shores with spray") to a final glimpse of "The
time-adorning monuments" which "Restore the secrets of eternity." Here, at the end of "The Statues," the "time-adorning
monuments" are certainly the images of the gods; but they are
also the figures of men who bravely admit their limited place in
time—and, just as certainly, they are all the works of art (such
as "The Statues" itself) which give order and meaning to
man's life.

The noble "anthropocentrism," to use Joseph Frank's term,[32]
dominant in "The Statues" is also at the center of "Colloquy
with a King-Crab" and "A Subject of Sea-Change," two other
poems making eloquent use of those sand and sea images which
imposed themselves on Bishop after he took up residence on
Cape Cod.

The blank-verse "Colloquy with a King-Crab" manages, within
the space of a relatively few lines, to comment cogently on the
double themes of the nature of poetry and of the unique place
of man in nature. The poem begins by enumerating some of the
particulars of the natural terrain, details which the poet feels
should provide "sufficient images / To say what [he has] sought."
Realizing, however, that an essential part of his task is "To know
what's sought from what the sands have found," the poet feels
it is his duty to impose human order on the landscape—to project
its details in a pattern that is transcendently meaningful. He is
not just a recorder, and he knows "It needs no Proteus to an-
nounce the sea / Above the proclamations of loud surf." For such
a role, even the horseshoe crab will do. At the same time, the
poet may not reject the crab, "Project of life, though hideous"—

the crab whose ugliness makes him "suspect" to the "imagination" even though his meaning is clear to the "abstract mind."

Finally, after the poet demonstrates to his imagination valid reasons for including the crab within a poem, he returns to a position stated earlier: that he may, perhaps must, use him in his poem, but may not yield to the temptation to be merely crablike in his poetry. Suddenly, new vistas open: the crab becomes an image of the sheer animality which man may transcend by giving order to the world in which he finds himself. The crab, once his significance is grasped, becomes a figure which man is tempted to imitate; but the brute existence of the scuttling creature ("His head all belly and his sword a tail") is not a proper end to be emulated by either the poet or man in general, even though neither poets nor mankind ought to ignore the meaning implicit within the crab's down-to-earth approach to life: "But his shell / Affords no edifice where I can creep / Though I consent like him to go on claws."

Bishop limns the posture proper to man, upright but wholly aware of his delimited place in time and the natural order, in "A Subject of Sea Change," a poem quite similar to "The Statues" in theme and outlook but very different in form and verse structure. The Phi Beta Kappa Poem for 1942, the work takes its title from the name of the house which Bishop had built on Cape Cod. A poem at the same time public and intensely personal, each of its four sections consists of a set of reflections prompted by images which greet the speaker as he gazes outward from the house to the shoreline and the incoming seas.

Rhyme is employed constantly in the poem, and throughout its four sections may be discovered a basic iambic pentameter structure. Bishop, however, frequently rings changes upon the metrics, and the rhymes are employed in a shifting and elusive manner. After the fairly definitive regularity of the opening sections, as seen in the initial stanza,

> I have built my house amid sea-bitten green,
> Among the pitch pines of a dispersed wood;
> The winters of five years it has withstood
> Incessant winds and in the salt air been
> Bleached in its shingles to a silvery grey,
> Which even now, when spring is overhead,
> Answers from thickets of unawakened bay

there occur such modulations as

> Here we are so far flung out
> Into the spacious seas, we cannot choose but know
> How all things come about and about.
> Sharper than any gale's tang on the cheek we feel
> Sensuously the seasonable wheel:
> Know the delayed spring's silvery advance
> And autumn's soon retiring golden rout
> Are largess in a long extravagance.

Set against the backdrop of World War II ("But then in the background I hear the great bombs drop"), "A Subject of Sea Change" is fully aware of the impermanence of history and man's mortality. At the same time, the poem hopefully projects images of order. In the end, the poem asserts Bishop's profound belief in the dignity of man as well as his belief that man may invest his life with meaning by assuming the burden of history and by taking upon himself the responsibility for his own conduct:

> I must learn again the great part of Man—
> Though the lines are scant that any man may speak—
> Proclaiming with such passion as I can
> The part first played, and nobly, by a Greek.
> Time is man's tragic responsibility
> And on his back he bears
> Both the prolific and destroying years.
> And so, I swear, he must surround each act
> With scruples that will hold intact
> Not merely his own, but human, dignity.

Once again, Bishop reminds his audience of a time when "There was a sea cast gods from its surf like spray" and says that "the need for order first created gods / Immortal, then gave them generation." Looking about him at the present state of civilization, when "now the world's confounded into odds / And state is mutilated or achieved," he insists upon the primacy of love, realized in passion; and he instructs his audience to remember how such passionate love once gave order to men's lives:

> Remember how Love came on the immediate swell
> Reflecting in a shiver of resplendent spray
> The dawn enclosed within her secret shell.
> No other god has held so visible a sway.

The poem concludes on a somber, if courageous, note, observing that "Death greets us all without civility / And every color of the sea is cold." But it also suggests that there are two possible ways of listening to the message of the sea: that of the hero who ventures to grasp its meaning; that of the dead who hear it too late. The second possibility is posited last, but the poem also makes clear to its readers the availability of the risk undertaken by Odysseus:

> And the sea rants,
> Storm-crossed, thunder-tossed,
> Yet has a poetry so profound
> That none but the unwaxed ear to the mast bound
> Should hear it, or it may be the lost
> Long-listening bodies of the drowned.

As a conclusion to this discussion of Bishop's poetry, an analysis more detailed than any yet attempted will be made of the 1941 elegy to F. Scott Fitzgerald. Although the imagery of the poem rises out of the Cape Cod landscape present in "The Statues" and "A Subject of Sea Change," "The Hours" has no close thematic affinities with the body of Bishop's work; consequently, a discussion of it may properly concentrate on matters of technique—in order to demonstrate the high degree of skill Bishop had attained to after thirty years' devotion to poetry. So that the reader may follow closely the analysis, the complete text of the poem is printed below:

THE HOURS

In the real dark night of the soul it is always three o'clock in the morning.—F. Scott Fitzgerald

I

All day, knowing you dead,
I have sat in this long-windowed room,
Looking upon the sea and, dismayed
By mortal sadness, though without thought to resume
Those hours which you and I have known—
Hours when youth like an insurgent sun
Showered ambition on an aimless air,
Hours foreboding disillusion,
Hours which now there is none to share.
Since you are dead, I leave them all alone.

II

A day like any day. Though any day now
We expect death. The sky is overcast,
And shuddering cold as snow the shoreward blast.
And in the marsh, like a sea astray, now
Waters brim. This is the moment when the sea
Being most full of motion seems motionless.
Land and sea are merged. The marsh is gone.
And my distress
Is at the flood. All but the dunes are drowned.
And brimming with memory I have found
All hours we ever knew, but have not found
The key. I cannot find the lost key
To the silver closet you as a wild child hid.

III

I think of all you did
And all you might have done, before undone
By death, but for the undoing of despair.
No promise such as yours when like the spring
You came, colors of jonquils in your hair,
Inspired as the wind, when the woods are bare
And every silence is about to sing.

None had such promise then, and none
Your scapegrace wit or your disarming grace;
For you were bold as was Danaë's son,
Conceived like Perseus in a dream of gold.
And there was none when you were young, not one,
So prompt in the reflecting shield to trace
The glittering aspect of a Gorgon age.

Despair no love, no fortune could assuage . . .
Was it a fault in your disastrous blood
That beat from no fortunate god,
The failure of all passion in mid-course?
You shrank from nothing as from solitude,
Lacking the still assurance, and pursued
Beyond the sad excitement by remorse.

Was it that having shaped your stare upon
The severed head of time, upheld and blind,
Upheld by the stained hair,
And seen the blood upon that sightless stare,
You looked and were made one
With the strained horror of those sightless eyes?
You looked, and were not turned to stone.

IV

You have outlasted the nocturnal terror,
The head hanging in the hanging mirror,
The hour haunted by a harrowing face.
Now you are drunk at last. And that disgrace
You sought in oblivious dives you have
At last, in the dissolution of the grave.

V

I have lived with you the hour of your humiliation.
I have seen you turn upon the others in the night
And of sad self-loathing
Concealing nothing
Heard you cry: *I am lost. But you are lower!*
And you had that right.
The damned do not so own their damnation.

I have lived with you some hours of the night,
The late hour
When the lights lower,
The later hour
When the lights go out,

When the dissipation of the night is past,
Hour of the outcast and the outworn whore,
That is past three and not yet four—
When the old blackmailer waits beyond the door
And from the gutter with unpitying hands
Demands the same sad guiltiness as before,
The hour of utter destitution
When the soul knows the horror of its loss
And knows the world too poor
For restitution,
           Past three o'clock
And not yet four—
             When not pity, pride,
Or being brave,
Fortune, friendship, forgetfulness of drudgery
Or of drug avails, for all has been tried,
And nothing avails to save
The soul from recognition of its night.

The hour of death is always four o'clock.
It is always four o'clock in the grave.

VI

Having heard the bare word that you had died,
All day I have lingered in this lofty room,
Locked in the light of sea and cloud,
And thought, at cost of sea-hours, to illume
The hours that you and I have known,
Hours death does not condemn, nor love condone.

And I have seen the sea-light set the tide
In salt succession toward the sullen shore
And while the waves lost on the losing sand
Seen shores receding and the sands succumb.

The waste retreats; glimmering shores retrieve
Unproportioned plunges; the dunes restore
Drowned confines to the disputed kingdom—
Desolate mastery, since the dark has come.

The dark has come. I cannot pluck you bays,
Though here the bay grows wild. For fugitive
As surpassed fame the leaves this sea-wind frays.
Why should I promise what I cannot give?

I cannot animate with breath
Syllables in the open mouth of death.
Dark, dark. The shore here has a habit of light.
O dark! I leave you to oblivious night!

In preparation for his poem, Bishop obviously re-read much
of Fitzgerald's work (the title and epigraph of the elegy are
derived from the observation in "The Crack-Up" that "in a real
dark night of the soul it is always three o'clock in the morning"[33]). The Bishop Papers at Princeton also reveal that he read
with care many previous elegies; and his detailed comments
upon "Lycidas" suggest that Milton's poem was influential in
shaping "The Hours." Although there are only a few direct echoes
of "Lycidas" and of the traditional characteristics of pastoral
elegy discernible in "The Hours," Milton's example probably
prompted Bishop to attempt a fairly long, complicated poem.
The multi-part structure and unequal line lengths are perhaps
partly indebted to Eliot, but there is also a precedent for such
structure and metrics in the digressive and irregular patterns of
the pastoral elegy.

For Bishop, Milton's example was particularly pertinent: he too was concerned with the formulation of a public statement of grief for a close friend who had been stricken in his prime. He, as well as Milton, saw his friend's fate as intimately linked with the evils and terrors of his age; and he too, because of the nature of his friend's ambition and endeavors, was driven to speculate about the precariousness of fame and earthly strivings. Bishop, like Milton, had to contend with personal grief; Bishop's situation, however, was more perplexing than that which Milton faced. Milton could approach his subject with a certain freedom because Edward King had died before either his poetic or pastoral talents could be conclusively demonstrated; Bishop's grief was complicated by his critical awareness that Fitzgerald's artistic gifts had been recklessly dissipated.

The opening section of "The Hours" is made up almost entirely of one long sentence which, when analyzed, seems hardly to be a sentence at all. It is, rather, a mosaic of utterances which establishes a mood of reflection and quiet grief. The first nine lines—in their calculated use of starts and stops, half sentences, and the repetition of the key word "hours"—closely approximate the structure of reminiscence and of unparticularized thought. The very arrangement of the words calls to mind the thought patterns of a man sitting all day looking out upon the sea and thinking of the past: "Hours which now there is none to share." Although of unequal syllabic length, the first nine lines all have four major stresses, with a full accent at the end of all but the seventh. The section's concluding line, which stresses the irrecoverability of the vanished hours of friendship, separates itself from the foregoing lines by a shift into strict iambic pentameter. At the same time, the last line is linked to those which have preceded it by means of a skillful echoing of the caesura and the ominous "dead" in the initial line. In addition, all ten lines are held together by an intricate rhyme scheme. Finally, if one accepts the proposition that the sounds of words may reinforce signific content, one may note that Bishop has consciously employed vowels and stressed nasals throughout the opening section as a means of subtly orchestrating the general mood of dismayed remembering.

In the second section, which presents images of the land and sea the poet views from his window, Bishop very gingerly adopts the pastoral convention of the pathetic fallacy. Although one is never told so explicitly, one receives the impression that nature in some fashion corresponds with the poet's grief: the sky is overcast; the tide is rising in the marsh. As the marsh is inundated, the poet realizes that his "distress / Is at the flood" and that he is "brimming with memory." Nature, however, is not able to provide him with "the lost key"[34] that will return him to the past and to a complete understanding of the forces which shaped his friend's career. In this section, the predominant metrical pattern is five-stress iambic; there is one shortened line, but it occurs at a point of natural division and emphasis. The rhyme pattern in this section is looser and less pronounced, but it functions well as a formal device to set off the verse stops in lines which display frequent enjambment.

Although the "wild child" in the last line of section two hints at Fitzgerald's character, only in the third section does one encounter detailed memories of the subject of the elegy—a reckoning with his achievements and undoing: "I think of all you did / And all you might have done, before undone / By death, but for the undoing of despair." While the comparison of Fitzgerald's early promise to the coming of spring, with "colors of jonquils in your hair," is perhaps flawed by a tinge of excessive sentiment, the simile does point up Fitzgerald's youthful vitality and it does contrast nicely with the earlier descriptions of the wintry landscape. In the second stanza, there is a happier comparison of Fitzgerald with "Danaë's son, / Conceived like Perseus in a dream of gold." The figure of Perseus suggests the heroic stature of Fitzgerald, "So prompt in the reflecting shield to trace / The glittering aspect of a Gorgon age"; but the "dream of gold" calls to mind the lust for fame and material success which so frequently misled and corrupted Fitzgerald's talents— even though he was partly aware of the tawdriness of such longings, of the "glittering aspect" of the "Gorgon age" in which he found his birth.

Bishop's praise of Fitzgerald's flawed heroism recalls his double observation in "The Missing All" that his friend's better work is devoted to a searching examination of the less prepossessing aspects of the American dream but that it is ultimately sapped by a failure of nerve. In the last two stanzas of section three, he once more asks what were the reasons for the overwhelming and fatal despair, the "failure of all passion in midcourse." Although the poet provides no explicit answers to his questions (as, in a poem, it is wise not to do), Bishop's analysis of Fitzgerald's shortcomings is quite similar to that which he had provided in the essay. The fault in Fitzgerald's "disastrous blood" was his "lacking the still assurance" once possessed by such Americans as Emily Dickinson but now dissipated in the ascetic withering of the Puritan tradition. It was both Fitzgerald's misfortune and his saving grace that, lacking the assurance of an Emily Dickinson, he was gifted with the insight and courage of a Perseus. His peculiar misfortune was that he could look upon the Gorgon's face and not be turned to stone—instead, he was maddened by the sightless horror of that face.

All four stanzas of this section are regularly composed of seven lines and all employ rhyme, but the line lengths are unequal and the rhymes are irregularly distributed. Although it might be supererogatory to comment upon each of the stanzas, a close look at the final one gives some notion of the technical brilliance of this section. The major portion of the stanza is in the form of a question: six lines of verse that slowly and delicately pace forward, by means of unobtrusive rhymes and the variation of five- and three-stress lines, to the final impact of "those sightless eyes," standing in unrhymed isolation at the climax of the verbal approximation of the slow, turning stare toward "the severed head of time." Then, the exquisitely drawn-out question is answered by the single line, with its most effective caesura, "You looked, and were not turned to stone."

At first glance, the brief fourth section might seem tastelessly vulgar, a bitter parody of the "consolation" traditionally proffered by the pastoral elegy. Bishop himself, however, held that "Any word may be used in a poem, provided it is resolved in the poem" (*CE*, 366). And the grisly puns in section four, the oblique references to hangovers, "oblivious dives," and the "dissolution of the grave" are resolved within the total structure of the poem. Just as the comic scenes in Shakespeare's tragedies provide a certain amount of breathing space in the mounting surge of the drama—as well as commentary from a different point of view on the major action of the drama—so does the fourth section of "The Hours" provide Bishop with an opportunity to alleviate and refocus his grief. The puns do not obviate his sorrow but make it more poignant and multidimensional; they are masks which enable Bishop to give voice both to the severity of his judgments and to the intensity of his emotions. Furthermore, such lines as "dissolution of the grave" and "Now you are drunk at last" may be interpreted in such a way that they do provide consolation: the lines undoubtedly refer to a sacramental union of the body with the earth. One should also keep in mind that these six lines are cast in quite strict five-stress iambic and that they employ a precise rhyme pattern; the formality of the verse definitely functions as a counterpoint to the seemingly callous nature of the statements themselves.

After the interlude provided by the short fourth section, the action of the poem again goes forward but with different emphasis and on a slightly different tack. The fifth section reverts to memories of the common past shared by the poet and the dead man, but now the memories are of hours of shared unhappiness and despair. This section, exploring the horrors of self-accusation and that insomniac stretch of the night when it is "Past three o'clock / And not yet four," strikes one as the least impressive part of the poem. Less rigidly formal than any other section, it is obviously designed to mediate between the tightly patterned structures of sections four and six. Bishop handles well the loose rhyme schemes and varying line lengths, but many of the lines are excessively prosaic and discursive. There is little vivifying imagery and not enough tension between the metrical substructure and the statements uttered by the speaker.

In the sixth and final section, Bishop returns to more formally ordered stanzas and very expertly employs meter, rhyme, and what he referred to as the "real" qualities of language. The sea and the movement of the tide and the coming of dusk function as images of the poet's final emotional complex—not overtly but as subtly sensuous renderings of states of feeling. Bishop again makes careful use of verbal overtones; long vowels and sonorous consonants are repeated in the rhyme words, and alliterative patterns of *s*'s and *d*'s are skillfully manipulated to suggest the sound and motion of the sea and the coming down of darkness: "the dunes restore / Drowned confines to the disputed kingdom— / Desolate mastery, since the dark has come."

There is in this last section a pitch of deep emotion—grief and a certain amount of despair and a sense of futility—but Bishop never approaches mawkishness or the poetic false note; and his success in this respect is largely due to his employment of strict verse. The verse provides a framework—a sense of the problem grappled and come to terms with—for the expression of emotion. In Bishop's own terms, the verse imposes a formal order on the disorder of being and thus makes that disorder not only intelligible but also somewhat supportable. Throughout the section, as the emotions become more intense, the verse becomes more formal; there is a tightening of form as the pitch of feeling is heightened. In the first three stanzas, there is no regular rhyme pattern, and the rhymes which do occur are apt to be off-rhymes. In the antepenultimate stanza, however, there is an *abab* pattern of exact rhymes; and in the last stanza the rhymes are once more precise, this time in an *aabb* pattern. Of course, one cannot really assert that this last pattern is more formal than the other, but there is a logical development toward the particular scheme of the last stanza. And there is appropriateness in Bishop's use of the couplet for the final statement of the poem:

> Dark, dark. The shore here has a habit of light.
> O dark! I leave you to oblivious night!

Bishop could not, as did Milton, hold out to his fame-questing friend the promise of a heavenly immortality; in his humility, he dared not even pluck earthly bays to crown the memory of the dissipated Fitzgerald. He could, however, offer his sympathy and his love; and he exerted all his skills and the full range of his careful craftsmanship in a successful effort to give voice to his affection. "The Hours" is one of the finest poems written in the twentieth century, a poem which admirably displays the mastery which its author had achieved after long dedication to his craft; it is also a poem which reveals the nobly human dimensions of John Peale Bishop.

CHAPTER 5

Conclusion

AFTER PUBLICATION of *The Collected Essays* and *The Collected Poems*, Stanley Edgar Hyman remarked that "Bishop is a rather more complex figure than we have tended to assume."[1] While few literary historians and critics have repeated Hyman's judgment in the past fifteen years, the complexities of Bishop's art are as discernible now as they were in the decade of his death—and the excellences of his work ought to be even more evident. Competent and insightful as a critic, arresting and forceful as an author of fiction, and richly various and masterful as a poet, Bishop should be known for all his work—and by more than a handful of contemporary American readers.

Although Bishop was not a particularly original critic and though his critical pieces do not articulate a grand design of principles and propositions, his essays and reviews always exhibit sound taste and good judgment. Bishop's speculations about mythology, his analyses of Southern culture and modern industrial society, his assertions of man's basic animality, his balanced praise of traditions and ordered societies, his careful notations on the techniques of art, his persistent demands that artistic craftsmanship be properly honored—all his views are as thought-provoking today as when he first set them down on paper. For the student of Bishop's fiction and poetry, the criticism ought to be particularly instructive; since the themes of the criticism are those of his more strictly creative work, familiarity with *The Collected Essays* casts light on the poems and stories.

Bishop's fictional output is small, but his one novel and his stories are worthy of praise both for their stylistic virtues and for their incisive commentaries on human nature. Bishop's fiction ranks high among that produced by Southern writers of the twentieth century. The cycle of short stories, *Many Thousands Gone*, is notable not only for its controlled panorama of Southern culture in its passage from ante-bellum dreams to turn-of-the-century decadence but also for its portraits of men and women reacting, predictably and unpredictably, to the stresses engendered by life on this earth. *Act of Darkness* is also valuable for its delineation of Southern society, but its major achievements are its rendering of the joys and terrors of adolescence and its perceptive examination of the paths into which human passions may betray themselves. The novels and the stories are the work of a man who had thought deeply about his subject matter and who had struggled earnestly to give shape to his thinking. Although Bishop's fiction is not without flaws, its virtues far outweigh its defects; it is more than regrettable that his novel and stories are even less well known than his criticism and poetry.

Although there is a preponderance of merit in Bishop's criticism and fiction, he will be chiefly remembered as a poet. He gave most of his energies to the art of poetry, and in this genre he achieved his most noteworthy accomplishments. In his early years he had difficulty in establishing an idiom identifiably his own; he nevertheless managed to produce a number of excellent poems during his long apprenticeship and his mature verse increasingly displays Bishop's own signature. A lyric poet endowed with a keenly attuned ear and a sensitive feel for language, Bishop was also a strong, vigorous artist. A meticulous craftsman, he was also a poet of substance. One of the most attractive features of Bishop's poetry is its variety of tone, structure, and form; he might have been eclectic, but he performed well in all the modes he essayed. Many of the commentators on Bishop's poetry have remarked—some of them a bit surprisedly—upon the number of genuinely memorable poems he created. The list of such poems varies from critic to critic, but I would put forward the following: "Speaking of Poetry," "Ode," "The Return," "Perspectives Are Precipices," "Counsel of Grief," "A Recollection," "The Tree," "Experience in the West," "The Saints," "The Hours," "A Subject of Sea Change," and "The Statues." All twelve are worthy of inclusion in any serious anthology of modern American poetry, and many other Bishop poems are only slightly less deserving of lasting fame.

Throughout the writing of this study, I have tried to keep on guard against the temptation to accord Bishop excessive praise; to my mind, one of the most reprehensible foibles of current literary scholarship is the unwarranted inflation of "neglected" writers. Bishop was not a "great" writer; he was, though, a good one. And I do think that his criticism, fiction, and poetry have been too lightly passed over in the generation since his death. Bishop's work—the whole of it—ought to be more widely known and more highly valued. The essays, stories, and poems brilliantly mirror John Peale Bishop's engaging and elusive personality—and what Mr. Hyman said of him in 1949 still holds: he was "a man imaginative, passionate, sensitive, dedicated to art, and deeply humanistic."[2]

Notes and References

Chapter One

1. The text of the first epitaph is to be found in Allen Tate's introduction to *The Collected Poems of John Peale Bishop* (New York, 1948), p. xvi; the text of the second (in Mrs. Bishop's hand) is among the Bishop Papers on deposit in the Dulles Memorial Library at Princeton University.

2. The biographical matter in this chapter has been gleaned from several sources. I have relied heavily on Edmund Wilson and Allen Tate's introductions to *The Collected Essays* and *The Collected Poems*, but I have also made extensive use of the Bishop Papers at Princeton. This material has also been graciously checked by Bishop's son, Jonathan Peale Bishop.

3. *The Collected Essays of John Peale Bishop*, edited by Edmund Wilson (New York, 1948), pp. 351-52.

4. F. Scott Fitzgerald, *This Side of Paradise* (New York, 1920), pp. 55-56.

5. To my knowledge, the longest mention of Bishop in a survey account of American fiction is a paragraph in Leslie Fiedler's latest apocalyptic vision. Fiedler holds that *Act of Darkness* is "the essential link between the Twenties novel of the South and more recent examples of Southern Gothic." *Waiting For the End* (New York, 1964), p. 37.

6. *Selected Poems of John Peale Bishop*, edited with an introduction by Allen Tate (London, 1960) p. ix.

7. M. L. Rosenthal, *The Modern Poets* (New York, 1960), p. 159.

8. Joseph Frank, "The Achievement of John Peale Bishop," *Minnesota Review*, II (1962), 325-44.

9. Robert W. Stallman, "The Poetry of John Peale Bishop," in *Southern Renascence*, edited by Louis D. Rubin and Robert D. Jacobs (Baltimore, 1953), pp. 368-91.

10. Horace Gregory and Marya Zaturenska, *A History of American Poetry 1900-1940* (New York, 1946), p. 458.

11. Edmund Wilson, *We Moderns* (catalogue of the Gotham Book Mart, n.d.), p. 14.

12. Joseph Frank, "Force and Form: A Study of John Peale Bishop," *Sewanee Review*, LV (1947), 106-7.

13. R. K. Meiners, "The End of History: Allen Tate's *Seasons of the Soul*," *Sewanee Review*, LXX (1962), 34-80.

14. Christian Gauss, "Edmund Wilson, The Campus, and the Nassau 'Lit'," *Princeton University Library Chronicle*, V (1943-44), 49-50.

15. Edmund Wilson, *The Shores of Light* (New York, 1952), p. 755.

16. F. Scott Fitzgerald, *The Crack-Up*, edited by Edmund Wilson (New York, 1945), p. 275.

17. Fred B. Millett, *Contemporary American Authors* (New York, 1940), p. 252.

Chapter Two

1. Joseph Frank, "Force and Form: A Study of John Peale Bishop," *Sewanee Review*, LV (1947), 71.
2. Bishop did, however, fully sympathize with the efforts of the Agrarians and with the principles they set forth in *I'll Take My Stand*.
3. See Tate's essay on Emily Dickinson in *Reactionary Essays on Poetry and Ideas* (New York, 1936), pp. 3-25.
4. See Henry Nash Smith, *Virgin Land: The American West as Myth and Symbol* (Cambridge, Mass., 1950).
5. Edmund Wilson, Introduction, *The Collected Essays*, p. ix.
6. Allen Tate, "A Note on Bishop's Poetry," *Southern Review*, I (1935), 363. Tate revised the text of his essay slightly when he published it in *Reactionary Essays;* although the changes are minor, I have used the *Southern Review* version because it was the one which prompted a long reply from Bishop.
7. See Joseph Campbell, *The Masks of God* (New York, 1959), particularly pp. 461-72.
8. Transcript, among the Bishop Papers at Princeton, of February 19, 1942, interview with Eve Merriam.
9. Tate, "A Note on Bishop's Poetry," p. 359.

Chapter Three

1. Letter of November 5, 1931.
2. Joseph Frank, "The Achievement of John Peale Bishop," *Minnesota Review*, II (1962), 327.
3. John Peale Bishop and Edmund Wilson, *The Undertaker's Garland* (New York, 1922), pp. 183-84.
4. *Story in America 1933-1934*, edited by Whit Burnett and Martha Foley (New York, 1934), p. 323.
5. *Southern Review*, I (1935), 61.
6. Cecil D. Elby, "The Fiction of John Peale Bishop," *Twentieth Century Literature*, VII (1961), 4-5.
7. *Many Thousands Gone* (New York, 1931), pp. 8-11.
8. Elby, *op. cit.*, pp. 5-6.
9. *Ibid.*, p. 7.
10. *Ibid.*, p. 9.
11. Additional support for my reading of this story is found in an essay on West Virginia which Bishop left uncompleted at his death. In the essay, the image of the underground caves recurs, and the passage makes quite clear that Bishop did not utterly reject the dissolution to which the Sabine sisters slowly yield: "The valley into which these Germans came lies between two ridges of strangely blue hills. Underneath are caves, arched between limestone and hollowed by a continual dripping. The dissolution of the stone has kept sweet a soil already rich" (*CE*, 457).
12. *Act of Darkness* (New York, 1935), pp. 357-58.
13. Letter of January 30, 1935.

14. Louis Rubin, "Southern Literature: The Historical Image," in *South: Modern Southern Literature in its Cultural Setting*, edited by Louis D. Rubin and Robert D. Jacobs (New York, 1961), p. 42.

Chapter Four

1. Allen Tate, "A Note on Bishop's Poetry," *Southern Review*, I (1935), 360; Horace Gregory and Marya Zaturenska, *A History of American Poetry 1900-1940*, p. 460.
2. Robert W. Stallman, "The Poetry of John Peale Bishop," in *Southern Renascence*, edited by Louis D. Rubin and Robert D. Jacobs (Baltimore, 1953), p. 371.
3. Tate, "A Note on Bishop's Poetry," p. 360.
4. Letter of January 12, 1936.
5. There is a similar comment in the "Aphorisms and Notes": "My imitation of other poets is in part a desire not to be myself" (*CE*, 374).
6. Tate, "A Note on Bishop's Poetry," p. 358.
7. *Ibid.*, p. 360.
8. "Symphony of a Mexican Garden," *Poetry*, I (October, 1912), 15.
9. "The Motive of the Magazine," *Poetry*, I (October, 1912), 28.
10. *The Nassau Literary Magazine*, LXX (December, 1914), 360.
11. *The Nassau Literary Magazine*, LXXII (April, 1916), 56.
12. *The Nassau Literary Magazine*, LXXII (May, 1916), 100.
13. *The Nassau Literary Magazine*, LXXII (January, 1917), 295-96.
14. *The Nassau Literary Magazine*, LXXII (March, 1917), 402-5.
15. Bishop would have known Eliot's early verse from its appearance in *Poetry;* he might also have encountered it in Pound's *A Catholic Anthology* (1915).
16. "Fragment," *Vanity Fair* (April, 1920), p. 12.
17. Babette Deutsch, *Poetry in Our Time*, second edition (New York, 1963), pp. 210-11.
18. *Vanity Fair* (September, 1920), pp. 61, 118.
19. For a thorough discussion of iconic verse in general, see Jean Hagstrum, *The Sister Arts* (Chicago, 1958), particularly pp. 17-18.
20. Mr. Tate informs me that both his poem and Bishop's were partly playful responses to Edmund Wilson's charge (in *The New Republic* of July, 1931) that Southern poets of the Agrarian persuasion were guilty of an excessive regard for their ancestors.
21. See Virginia Rock's dissertation, "The Making and Meaning of *I'll Take My Stand:* A Study in Utopian Conservatism, 1925-1939" (University of Minnesota, 1961), pp. 333-34, for information about the composition and initial publication of the poem.
22. Tate, "A Note on Bishop's Poetry," p. 362.
23. *Ibid.*
24. There are even verbal parallels between the verse and the essays; publication dates suggest, however, that the poems were composed prior to the essays.
25. Introduction to *Selected Poems of John Peale Bishop* (London, 1960), p. vii.

26. Jessie L. Weston, *From Ritual to Romance*, Anchor Books edition (New York, 1957), p. 89.

27. *Ibid.*, p. 88.

28. Joseph Frank, "The Achievement of John Peale Bishop," *Minnesota Review*, II (1962), 339.

29. *Ibid.*, p. 340.

30. For the text of the last two poems, see "Some Unpublished Poems of John Peale Bishop," *Sewanee Review*, LXXI (1963), 527-37. Subsequent references to poems appearing in the 1963 *Sewanee Review* (*SR*) will be indicated parenthetically within the text.

31. The entire passage (*CE*, 167), translated from *La crise de l'esprit*, casts light upon "The Statues":

> We have heard tell of whole worlds that have disappeared, of empires that have foundered with all their men and all their engines; gone straight down to the inexorable bottom of the centuries, with their gods and their laws, their academies and their sciences, both pure and applied, with their grammars, their dictionaries, their classics, their romantics and their symbolists, their critics and the critics of their critics. We have seen through the profound depths of history the phantoms of immense ships, which had once borne wealth and intelligence.... And we see now that the abyss of history is big enough for everybody.

32. Joseph Frank, "The Achievement of John Peale Bishop," p. 343.

33. F. Scott Fitzgerald, *The Crack-Up*, p. 75.

34. The "lost key" is an allusion to *Tender Is the Night*. See Book 2, chapter vi, of the 1934 text of the novel.

Chapter Five

1. Stanley Edgar Hyman, "Notes on the Organic Unity of John Peale Bishop," *Accent*, IX (1949), 113.

2. *Ibid.*

Selected Bibliography

PRIMARY SOURCES

I. Books

Green Fruit. Boston: Sherman, French & Company, 1917.
The Undertaker's Garland (in collaboration with Edmund Wilson). New York: Alfred A. Knopf, Inc., 1922.
Many Thousands Gone. New York: Charles Scribner's Sons, 1931.
Now With His Love. New York: Charles Scribner's Sons, 1933.
Minute Particulars. New York: The Alcestis Press, 1935.
Act of Darkness. New York: Charles Scribner's Sons. 1935.
Selected Poems. New York: Charles Scribner's Sons, 1941.
The Collected Poems of John Peale Bishop. Edited with an Introduction by ALLEN TATE. New York: Charles Scribner's Sons, 1948.
The Collected Essays of John Peale Bishop. Edited with an Introduction by EDMUND WILSON. New York: Charles Scribner's Sons, 1948.
Selected Poems of John Peale Bishop. Edited with an Introduction by ALLEN TATE. London: Chatto and Windus, 1960.

II. Significant Uncollected Pieces

"Fragment" (poem). *Vanity Fair* (April, 1920), p. 12.
"The Golden Age of the Dandy" (essay). *Vanity Fair* (September, 1920), pp. 61, 118.
"The Art of Living as a Feminine Institution" (essay). *Vanity Fair* (November, 1920), pp. 47, 116.
"America Becomes 'Past' Conscious" (essay). *Vanity Fair* (February, 1925), pp. 25-26.
"The New Mother Goose" (verse). *Vanity Fair* (July, 1925), p. 23.
"The Fireplace" (story). *Story*, III (November, 1933), 64-72.
"A Man Who Thought" (story). *Southern Review*, I (July, 1935), 58-65.
"Some Unpublished Poems of John Peale Bishop." Edited with an Introduction by ROBERT L. WHITE. *Sewanee Review*, LXXI (Autumn 1963). 527-37.

SECONDARY SOURCES

I. Background Material

BRADBURY, JOHN M. *The Fugitives: A Critical Account.* Chapel Hill: University of North Carolina Press, 1958. (See comment below.)
COWAN, LOUISE. *The Fugitive Group.* Baton Rouge: Louisiana State University Press, 1959. Both the Bradbury and Cowan books contain excellent discussions of the Southern writers with whom Bishop was most in sympathy.

Selected Bibliography

COWLEY, MALCOLM. *Exile's Return.* Second edition. New York: W. W. Norton & Company, 1951. The rightly famous account, by one who was there, of the expatriate movement of the 1920's and 1930's.

DEUTSCH, BABETTE. *Poetry in Our Time.* Second Edition. New York: Doubleday Anchor Books, 1963. Though not a formal history, still the best account of modern British and American poetry. Contains a favorable discussion of Bishop's verse.

FILLER, LOUIS (ed.). *The Anxious Years.* New York: G. P. Putnam's Sons, 1963. A stimulating anthology, its emphasis slightly to the left, of American writing in the 1930's.

GAUSS, CHRISTIAN. "Edmund Wilson, The Campus, and The 'Lit'," *Princeton University Library Chronicle,* V (1944), 41-50. An attempt, by Bishop's most influential teacher, to recapture the Princeton literary scene during the years when Bishop was a student.

GIBSON, ROBERT (ed.). *Modern French Poets on Poetry.* Cambridge: Cambridge University Press, 1961. An excellent anthology of critical pronouncements by writers who exerted a lasting influence on Bishop.

GREGORY, HORACE and MARYA ZATURENSKA. *A History of American Poetry 1900-1940.* New York: Harcourt, Brace and Company, 1946. A partisan history which contains an unfavorable estimate of Bishop.

HOFFMAN, FREDERICK J. *The Twenties.* Second edition. New York: Collier Books, 1962. Best literary history of the period. Contains a few references to Bishop.

JOSEPHSON, MATTHEW. *Life Among the Surrealists.* New York: Holt, Rinehart and Winston, 1962. Lively memories of American and European literary activities during the 1920's and 1930's.

RUBIN, LOUIS D. and ROBERT D. JACOBS (eds.). *South: Modern Southern Literature in Its Cultural Setting.* New York: Doubleday Dolphin Books, 1961. Twenty-one essays, most of them good, on various subjects and authors. Louise Cowan's essay on modern Southern poetry contains a brief discussion of "Experience in the West."

WILSON, EDMUND. *The Shores of Light: A Literary Chronicle of the Twenties and Thirties.* New York: Farrar, Strauss and Young, 1952. A brilliant panorama of the period. Contains occasional references to Bishop.

II. *Works specifically about Bishop*

ARROWSMITH, WILLIAM. "An Artist's Estate," *Hudson Review,* II (1949), 118-27. Lucid summary of Bishop's career, and an earnest attempt to understand his work against the backdrop of modern literature in general.

ASTERLUND, B. "John Peale Bishop," *Wilson Library Bulletin,* XVIII (1944), 424. Biographical sketch.

BIER, JESSIE. "A Critical Biography of John Peale Bishop." Doctoral dissertation, Princeton University, 1956. Although saddled with the general thesis that Bishop's work consistently reflects a Spenglerian view of history, this dissertation contains a great deal of biographical data and excellent analyses of individual works.

——. "John Peale Bishop: The Memory Lingers On," *Western Humanities*

Review, IX (1955), 243-48. A redaction of Bier's dissertation conclusion.

ELBY, CECIL D., JR. "The Fiction of John Peale Bishop," *Twentieth Century Literature,* VII (1961), 3-9. Argues that Bishop's fiction is motivated by a rejection of the myth of the South. Focuses on *Many Thousands Gone.*

FRANK, JOSEPH. "The Achievement of John Peale Bishop," *Minnesota Review,* II (1962), 325-44. Stresses the mythological dimensions of Bishop's work. Excellent comment on the later poetry.

————. "Force and Form: A Study of John Peale Bishop," *Sewanee Review,* LV (1947), 71-107. Discusses Bishop's work in the light of his efforts to reconcile the opposites in human temperament and history. Frank's two essays are essential for the student of Bishop.

HYMAN, STANLEY EDGAR. "Notes on the Organic Unity of John Peale Bishop," *Accent,* IX (1949), 102-13. Stresses the complexity and richness of Bishop's criticism and poetry.

PATRICK, J. MAX and ROBERT W. STALLMAN. "John Peale Bishop: A Checklist," *Princeton University Library Chronicle,* VII (1946), 62-79. A generally complete bibliography of Bishop's published writings.

STALLMAN, ROBERT W. "*A Recollection,*" *The Explicator,* XIX (April, 1961), item 43. Argues that by means of the acrostic Bishop privately ridicules his own style.

————. "John Peale Bishop," *Western Review,* XI (1946), 5-19. An early version of the essay noted below.

————. "The Poetry of John Peale Bishop," in *Southern Renascence,* edited by LOUIS D. RUBIN and ROBERT D. JACOBS. Baltimore: John Hopkins University Press, 1953, pp. 368-91. A disorderly essay valuable for its checklist of Bishop criticism and for its remarks on the structure of Bishop's poetry.

TATE, ALLEN. "A Note on Bishop's Poetry," *Southern Review,* I (1935), 357-64. (Reprinted in *Reactionary Essays.*) Perceptive assessment of the poetry of Bishop's middle years; still valuable for comments on individual poems.

WILSON, EDMUND. "John Peale Bishop," *We Moderns.* Catalogue of the Gotham Book Mart, n.d. A brief estimate.

Index

Index

Note: titles of poems receiving only passing notice in the text are not included in the index.